PROTECTING *your*
ASSETS

---

from PROBATE

---

and LONG-TERM

CARE

PROTECTING *your* ASSETS

from PROBATE

and LONG-TERM

CARE

**DON'T LET
THE SYSTEM
BANKRUPT
YOU AND YOUR
LOVED ONES**

EVAN H. FARR

**ALLWORTH
PRESS**

Allworth Press books may be purchased in bulk at special discounts for sales promotion, corporate gifts, fund-raising, or educational purposes. Special editions can also be created to specifications. For details, contact the Special Sales Department, Allworth Press, 307 West 36th Street, 11th Floor, New York, NY 10018 or info@skyhorsepublishing.com.

20 19   7 6

Published by Allworth Press, an imprint of Skyhorse Publishing, Inc.
307 West 36th Street, 11th Floor, New York, NY 10018.

Allworth Press® is a registered trademark of Skyhorse Publishing, Inc.®, a Delaware corporation.

www.allworth.com

Cover design by Mary Belibasakis

Library of Congress Cataloging-in-Publication Data is available on file.

Print ISBN: 978-1-62153-553-9
Ebook ISBN: 978-1-62153-562-1

Printed in the United States of America

Table of Contents

Foreword

Most people doing estate planning use a revocable living trust to avoid the hassles and expenses of probate. There are hundreds of books and thousands of websites devoted to the revocable living trust, and it is widely recognized by attorneys and consumers that a revocable living trust is tremendously superior to a last will and testament as an estate planning tool. This book will not attempt to explore in depth all of the benefits of a revocable living trust, but it will highlight some. Readers not familiar with all of the benefits of a revocable living trust should obtain one of the many other excellent books on this topic.

One of the best is the seminal book on the topic—*The Living Trust: The Failproof Way to Pass Along Your Estate to Your Heirs* by Henry Abst. Mr. Abst essentially created the revocable living trust industry when he published his book back in 1989, which quickly became and still is the "bible" on how to avoid probate. I remember it, because I started practice back in 1987, two years before his book came out, and at that time no one was doing living trusts; they were essentially unheard of. Even though living trusts had been used as far back as sixteenth-century England, Mr. Abst came along just twenty-five years ago, put together all the puzzle pieces, wrote a book explaining it, and completely revolutionized the estate planning industry.

Although a revocable living trust does a terrific job of avoiding probate, what most people don't realize is that a revocable living trust does not protect your assets from creditors or from the expenses of long-term care.

What Mr. Abst did for the revocable living trust, I have done for the Living Trust Plus™—revolutionizing the estate planning and asset protection industry since 2009 by making the Living Trust Plus a nationally recognized estate planning option—the only option that provides consumers with all the best features of a regular living trust *plus* the extra and vital benefit of asset protection that consumers are so hungry for.

This book will explain, among other things, how to use the Living Trust Plus to protect your assets from the expenses of probate *plus* lawsuits *plus* long-term care. In doing so, I will first explain the problems of probate and the risks of lawsuits and long-term care. Then we'll start looking at the possible solutions. First, we'll look at whether wills offer a solution. Second, we'll look at joint ownership and beneficiary designations. Third, we'll examine living trusts—both the regular living trust (i.e., the revocable living trust that Mr. Abst wrote about and that almost everybody has heard of, designed primarily to avoid probate) and, more important, the Living Trust Plus. Last, we'll explore numerous other solutions that will protect your assets from the expenses of probate and long-term care.

—**Evan H. Farr, CELA, CAP**
Certified Elder Law Attorney,
National Elder Law Foundation
Member, Council of Advanced Practitioners, NAELA
Creator of the Living Trust Plus™
www.LivingTrustPlus.com
www.FarrLawFirm.com
EverythingElderLaw.com

CHAPTER 1

The Problem of Probate

Almost everyone has heard of "the nightmare of probate." These words just go together. You hardly ever hear about probate without hearing about the "nightmare of probate" because probate really is, for the most part, almost always a nightmare.

Basically, probate is a complex, expensive, court-supervised process that many families are forced to go through when a loved one becomes incapacitated during his or her lifetime, or when a loved one dies. Probate occurs whether your loved one becomes incapacitated and does not have a general power of attorney, or dies without a will (intestate), or dies with a will (testate). Consider the following case study.

PROBATE CASE STUDY

Background

Mary Johnson is an eighty-four-year-old widow with three children—Joan, Sam, and Bill. Joan and Sam are both trustworthy and responsible adults and have maintained a loving relationship with Mary over the years. Joan is a nurse in a doctor's office, and Sam works as an advertising executive. Bill, unfortunately, has had a checkered past—he's never held a job for more than a year, has had serious financial problems, has spent time in jail for theft (including stealing a significant sum of money from Mary), and has had no contact with the rest of the family for the past fifteen years.

Mary's husband, John, died three years ago. John died intestate, meaning he had never written a will, and when he died, his estate had to go into probate because John had several accounts that did not have Mary's name on them. Mary had paid a lawyer more than $10,000 to have John's estate probated so all of John's accounts could be put into her name, and Mary didn't want her children to have to go through all that hassle and expense when she died.

So Mary asked the lawyer to draw up a will for her, assuming that the will would avoid the expenses and hassles of probate that she had gone through with John's estate. She told the attorney to name her children Joan and Sam as the beneficiaries of her will and to name Joan to be the executor of her will. Because Mary didn't want to leave anything to Bill, she didn't bother mentioning Bill to the attorney. At the attorney's suggestion, Mary also signed incapacity planning documents—a general power of attorney and an advance medical directive. The lawyer explained that these documents were important for avoiding lifetime probate if Mary were to become incapacitated. Unfortunately, the lawyer did not explain that Mary's will would simply put her estate through probate after her death because he just assumed Mary understood that.

Mary was very pleased to tell Joan and Sam that she had set up everything with the lawyer to make things as easy as possible for Joan and Sam after her death, not realizing that the will she signed was *not* going to avoid probate, but rather was going to put her estate through probate.

One year after her husband's death, Mary fell and broke her hip, an extremely common occurrence among women Mary's age. After undergoing hip surgery, Mary spent four days in the hospital and was then transferred to a nearby nursing facility for rehabilitation. At first, Mary did the best she could to participate in all of the exercises the physical therapists wanted her to do. But then, about two weeks after the surgery, Mary developed pneumonia, a very serious complication after major surgery, and she was so weakened after contracting pneumonia that she felt unable to participate in the physical therapy.

Tragically, Mary's condition continued to worsen, and her weakened condition led to her not being able to leave the nursing home. As happens to so many elders, Mary wound up staying at the nursing home and simply transitioning from short-term rehabilitation into long-term care. Although she recovered from the pneumonia, Mary never regained her strength, and her condition slowly deteriorated over the ensuing months and years. After almost three years in the nursing home, Mary fell again and broke the same hip she had broken previously. After being hospitalized and undergoing another surgery, Mary again developed pneumonia and also suffered some additional complications from the surgery. This time, Mary was too weak to recover from the surgery and all of the complications. She died just one week after the surgery.

The First Step in Probate: A Trip to the Courthouse

After Mary's death, Joan makes an appointment to see the attorney who handled her father's estate and drew up her mother's will. Joan is horrified to find out that Mary's will must be admitted to probate.

Mary's assumption that a will would avoid probate (an assumption shared by Joan) was completely wrong. The attorney explains that the whole purpose of a will is to give instructions to the probate court. A will, the attorney explained correctly, doesn't even become effective until it's accepted by the probate court as valid and admitted to probate, thereby commencing the probate process.

The probate process differs from state to state, and the process is more complicated in some states than others. This story is an example of the probate process in Virginia.

Disgusted with the attorney for never explaining all of this to her mother, Joan decides to handle the probate process herself. She takes her mother's will and death certificate to the courthouse and sits down to talk to the probate clerk for an hour or two, filling out lots of forms and answering lots of questions. The end result of this initial courthouse visit is that Joan gets a certificate stating that she has been officially appointed by the court as the executor of Mary's will, along with a three-inch-thick manila envelope full of forms and instructions, statutes and samples, explaining all her duties as the executor of Mary's estate.

To fulfill her duties, Joan will have to complete and file a lot of legal forms with the probate court. Some are relatively easy; others, as Joan will soon find out, are incredibly complicated.

The Real-Estate Wait

One of the first things Joan wants to do is clean out Mary's house and get it ready for sale. Joan contacts a cleaning company, a moving company, and an auction company to deal with all of Mary's household belongings. Then she hires a real estate agent and lists the house for sale. At the closing on the sale of the house, Joan is dismayed to learn that the net proceeds from the sale of the house will have to be held in escrow by the title company for a year before the proceeds can actually be paid to the estate. This is because of a state law that says the proceeds from the sale of real estate are subject to debts of the estate for a one-year period.

The Probate-Filing Fiasco

Joan's visit to the probate court was just the beginning of a lengthy, complex, tedious, and expensive process. Now that she's gone to court and been appointed as the executor of her mother's will, she needs to start filling out and filing all of the required legal documents.

Notices to Ne'er-Do-Wells

The first thing Joan needs to file is the notice to heirs. Joan is again horrified—this time to find out from the court clerk that the term "heirs" includes her brother Bill. Even though Mary did not leave anything to Bill, Mary's heirs are all of her children (Bill included) because her heirs are the people who would inherit her estate if she had died without a will. The court clerk explains to Joan that the state has written a simple will for everyone that says if your spouse has predeceased you, then "everything goes to your children in equal shares." So even though Mary intended to disinherit Bill, he is still one of her heirs, and because her estate has wound up in probate, Bill must be notified that Mary died. Worse yet, once Bill receives that notice, he'll be given ample opportunity to contest her will.

The Illusive Inventory

After sending the notices to all of the heirs and filing an affidavit with the probate court certifying that she sent the notices, Joan must file a second legal document with the probate court, called an inventory of the estate. The inventory is due four months after Joan first went to court to become the executor of her mother's estate. The inventory Joan must file is an itemized listing of all the assets that Mary owned as of the date of her death and the exact value of all those assets as of that date. For Mary's real estate, that means getting an appraisal. Mary's financial assets were a checking account and a savings account with her local bank, a brokerage account, a money market account, a certificate of deposit, and one hundred shares of stock in the Arlington Community Bank that Mary's husband had purchased more than thirty years earlier. Adding all of her financial assets to the value of Mary's real estate, Mary died with an estate worth approximately $300,000. Her estate would have been almost double that except that Mary's three years in the nursing home had cost almost $100,000 per year.

For each financial asset, Joan writes the financial institution to ask for the exact value of every asset as of the date of death. After six months, the financial institution holding the money market account still hasn't responded, and Joan remains unable to determine what to do about the bank stock because the bank in question hasn't existed for at least twenty-five years, having been the subject of numerous mergers and acquisitions over the years.

About eighteen months and dozens of hours of research later, Joan finally determines which "megabank" is the successor to the old bank stock, but when Joan contacts the megabank, they tell her they'll have to do their own research to figure out how much the stock is worth. Another eighteen months will go by, and Joan will still have heard nothing from the bank about the stock.

After another number of months, Joan will have also written five letters and made half a dozen phone calls to the institution holding the money market and will still never have gotten the date of death value of the money market, meaning that even after three years from Mary's death, Joan still won't be able to finalize the inventory or close the probate estate.

The Abhorrent Accounting

But wait—it gets worse! Joan must start filing accountings with the probate court sixteen months after the probate process began, and then annually every year after that. This must be done despite the fact that Joan has not been able to finalize the inventory of the estate. It's the annual accounting that's the most complex part of probate, and primarily what gives the term "nightmare" to the phrase "nightmare of probate."

Conceptually, doing an accounting is similar to balancing your checkbook. Sometimes it balances; sometimes it doesn't. When your checkbook doesn't balance, how much time do you spend trying to figure out where the mistake was made? Often, if it's a small error, you'll decide it's not worth your time to hunt down the error, so you make an adjustment and you move on.

With a probate court accounting, the court will not accept the accounting unless it balances to the penny. Although you balance your checkbook for just one bank account and one month at a time, a probate accounting typically involves numerous accounts and is for a twelve-month period.

Joan spends over sixty hours initially preparing the first accounting for Mary's estate, and when she's done, she finds there's a $3.42 discrepancy. Sadly, she must now go back through all fifty-two bank statements (twelve for the checking account, twelve for the savings account, twelve for the brokerage account, twelve for the money market account, and four for the certificate of deposit) to try to track down the $3.42 error.

Did Joan make a math mistake, or did one of the bank's optical scanners make the mistake—misreading a 5 as a 2, or an 8 as a 3? Was it a single mistake or was it actually multiple smaller mistakes? After spending another tortuous ninety hours scrutinizing every bank statement, she finally finds the two bank errors and is able to submit the first of many annual accountings she will be filing.

The Will War
Because probate is a court-supervised process, it is very easy for a disgruntled heir to come along and contest a will. This is exactly what Bill did when he received the legal notice from his sister Joan about his mom having died and then found out that he was not mentioned in the will.

Bill didn't even hire a lawyer, because he couldn't afford one. All he did was write a letter, file it at the courthouse, and ask for a hearing. Joan didn't bother getting a lawyer, either, because she figured her mom's will was very clear in leaving the estate only to Joan and Sam.

At the hearing, the Judge looked at the will, saw that Bill wasn't mentioned, and decided that Bill was therefore entitled to one-third of his mother's estate. Joan was of course dumbstruck. Why did this happen? Because the law considered Bill to be a "forgotten heir"—the child of a person who has written a will in which the child is not left anything and is not mentioned at all. After the death of a parent, a forgotten heir has the right to demand the share that he would have received as an heir under the laws of intestacy. The reasoning is that the law presumes the parent either inadvertently forgot the child or incorrectly believed the child was dead, and did not mean to leave him out.

The Expenses of Probate

The executor of an estate is either going to spend a lot of time herself doing everything that needs to be done, or else she is going to spend a lot of money hiring an attorney to do it for her. In connection with Mary's estate, after three years, Joan estimates that she's already spent more than four hundred hours dealing with the court; dealing with the financial institutions; preparing and filing the required notices, inventory, and accountings; and dealing with her brother's will contest in court. At $25 per hour, which is how much Joan makes as a nurse, she calculates she has spent more than $10,000-worth of her time dealing with her mother's probate estate.

Had Joan hired a lawyer to do all of the work, she probably would have spent $10,000 to $15,000. And these numbers don't even include the various filing fees and probate taxes in connection with probate. Typical estimates for the costs associated with probate put the number at around 5 to 8 percent of the estate per year, so for a $300,000 estate such as Mary's, the average costs associated with probate would be approximately $15,000 to $24,000 per year, and this doesn't include estate taxes, income taxes, or litigation expenses that may be due during the course of the probate. Typical costs are broken down into many different categories.

Court Costs and Filing Fees

These costs and fees are dictated by state law and can range anywhere from a few hundred dollars to a few thousand dollars per year.

Bond Fees

If you don't have a will, or if the will doesn't waive the posting of a bond by your personal representative, then in most states your personal representative will have to pay for a surety bond in an amount determined by the probate court in order to be appointed as personal representative. Some states don't allow waiver of bond in some situations, such as when there are minor beneficiaries of the estate.

Appraisal and Business Valuation Fees

Appraisals will be necessary to determine the date of death values of certain assets, such as real estate and businesses. Many states also require date of death value of tangible personal property items such as jewelry, furniture, art work, and vehicles. Appraisal fees can range anywhere from a few hundred to a few thousand dollars, while business valuation fees will typically run several thousand dollars.

Attorney Fees

Legal fees are generally subject to state oversight or controlled by state law. They may be calculated in the same manner as the personal representative's fee, or be taken out of the personal representative's fee, or be in addition to the personal representative's fee, depending on what services the attorney is providing. If the attorney is performing the duties normally performed by the personal representative, then the attorney's fee will probably be taken out of the personal representative's fee. However, if the attorney is handling purely legal matters, such as litigation, that the personal representative could not be expected to handle alone, then the attorney's fees will typically be in addition to the personal representative's fee.

Accountant Fees

Fees for an accounting firm will vary with each estate and may depend upon the value of the estate and the type of assets owned. A small estate that contains a lot of different accounts may cost more in accounting fees than a larger estate that owns just a few assets. Accountants are often enlisted to prepare and file the final tax return of the decedent and to help prepare the annual accountings of an estate (although an attorney may perform these services as well). If the estate itself is a large estate that has to pay estate taxes (either to the state and/or to the federal government), then the accounting fees will include the preparation and filing of the appropriate estate tax returns. Again, the attorney for the estate may prepare and file these tax returns.

Miscellaneous Fees

Miscellaneous costs and fees can include items such as the cost of postage to mail notices to the heirs at law (the people who would inherit your estate if you died without a will) and to the named beneficiaries of the will, fees to a search firm to track down beneficiaries whose whereabouts are unknown, fees to file documents with the court, probate and recording taxes, insurance costs, storage costs, and costs to ship or move tangible personal property.

Creditor Claims

Another problem of probate is that creditors typically have a long time (up to five years in Virginia) to file a claim or a lawsuit against the estate, or to go after the beneficiaries of the estate. Joan wasn't worried about creditors because Joan had Mary's power of attorney and had been taking care of paying Mary's bills for the past three years while Mary was in the nursing home, and Joan "knew" that all of Mary's bills had been paid.

What Joan didn't know was that right after being notified of Mary's death, Joan's brother broke into Mary's house, stole three of her credit cards, and charged $45,000 on those cards. Bill also had his girlfriend, pretending to be Joan, call up the credit card companies and change the mailing address on the cards, so Mary never saw the statements come in. Mary had never bothered to cancel the credit cards because she "knew" they had no outstanding balance.

About fifteen months passed before the credit card company contacted Joan by phone and told her of the outstanding balance. By then, Joan had distributed almost all of the money from the estate to herself and her two siblings, so the estate didn't have enough money left to pay off the credit cards. Joan figured out what happened and told the credit card company to go after her brother Bill and his girlfriend, which it did, but the credit card company had no luck finding Bill or his girlfriend. So after about another eighteen months, the credit card company sued Mary's estate, and they also sued Joan and Sam as beneficiaries of the estate, since Joan and Sam had already received most of their distributions from the estate. Even though Bill was the one who stole and used the credit cards, Joan and Sam were the ones who got stuck paying.

Conclusion

This case study only deals with postmortem (i.e., after-death) probate. Equally onerous is the process of lifetime probate that occurs when someone becomes incapacitated during his or her lifetime and does not have a proper power of attorney in place. Mary's story is just one of hundreds of thousands of probate horror stories that occur every day. It provides a summary of the main problems of probate, and why so many people want to avoid it by doing incapacity planning to avoid lifetime probate and by doing estate planning to avoid postmortem probate.

CHAPTER 2

The Problem of Long-Term Care

Chapter 1 explained some of the problems associated with probate. Now, let's switch gears and talk about the problem of long-term care.

Whether you're rich, poor, or somewhere in between, you cannot afford to ignore the potentially devastating costs of nursing home care and other types of long-term care.

First of all, what is meant by long-term care? We're talking about what is also called custodial care, where people need assistance with the activities of daily living— bathing, eating, dressing, going to the bathroom—your basic human needs. Many people who need long-term care also need assistance with the instrumental activities of daily living such as cooking, cleaning, taking care of household chores, paying bills, taking care of pets—not quite the basic human needs, but pretty essential for someone to be able to live independently on their own. So once people need help with these things, they need long-term care; however, the degrees of long-term care vary.

A lot of people also need long-term care because of dementia. Almost everybody knows someone with Alzheimer's disease or some other form of dementia. Alzheimer's disease is the third leading cause of death in the United States. Of course, before it causes death, it causes people to lose their memory and their ability to handle their own activities of daily living. Some sufferers of Alzheimer's have physical problems; many have no significant physical problems at all but simply have lost their memory. They have forgotten how to eat and bathe and dress and brush their teeth and do anything to care for themselves. They might be able to do these things with somebody standing next to them and guiding them every step of the way, but they wouldn't do anything if they didn't have constant supervision and reminders.

Nursing homes are the most likely and one of the most expensive creditors that you are likely to face in your lifetime. Consider the following statistics:

- About 70 percent of Americans who live to age sixty-five will need long-term care at some time in their lives, over 40 percent in a nursing home.[1]
- As of 2012, the national average cost of a private room in a nursing home was $248 per day, or $90,520 per year, and the national average cost of a semiprivate room was $222 per day, or $81,030 per year.[2]
- On average, someone age sixty-five today will need some long-term care services for three years. Women need care for longer (on average 3.7 years) than do men (on average 2.2 years). While about one-third of today's sixty-five-year-olds may never need long-term care ser-

[1] National Clearinghouse for Long-Term Care Information, http://www.longtermcare.gov at Home > Understanding LTC > Definitions & Need for LTC > Will You Need LTC?

[2] The 2012 MetLife Market Survey of Nursing Home, Assisted Living, Adult Day Services, and Home Care Costs, at http://tinyurl.com/MetLife-Survey2012.

vices, 20 percent of them will need care for more than five years.[3]

- Also, long-term care is not just needed by the elderly. A recent study by Unum Insurance found that 46 percent of its group long-term care claimants were under the age of sixty-five at the time of disability.[4]

Contrast the previous long-term care statistics with statistics for automobile accident claims and homeowner's insurance claims:

- In any given year, an average of only 7.6 percent of insured vehicle owners file an automobile insurance claim.[5]
- In any given year, an average of only 5.78 percent of people per year filed a claim on their homeowner's insurance.[6]

Almost everyone who drives has auto insurance, and almost everyone who owns a home has homeowner's insurance, yet only about 10 percent of the population has long-term care insurance. The other 90 percent are totally at risk for winding up financially destitute because of the need for nursing home care.

---

[3] The 2012 MetLife Market Survey of Nursing Home, Assisted Living, Adult Day Services, and Home Care Costs, at http://tinyurl.com/MetLife-Survey2012.

[4] Insurance Information Institute, http://www.iii.org/media/facts/statsbyissue/longtermcare.

[5] Insurance Institute for Highway Safety, http://www.iihs.org/research/hldi/fact_sheets/CollisionLoss_0910.pdf, based on data from the Highway Loss Data Institute.

[6] Insurance Institute for Highway Safety, http://www.iii.org/media/facts/statsbyissue/homeowners, based on data from the Insurance Services Office.

If you're one of the 90 percent of people who have not purchased long-term care insurance, what are your options for paying for long-term care? The best time for you to address this question is when you do your estate planning. It is estimated that only 30 percent of Americans do estate planning—an absurdly low percentage—but this is still three times greater than the percentage of people who purchase long-term care insurance. The reason you should address the problem of long-term care while doing estate planning is that the best estate plan in the world won't matter a bit if all of your money is wiped out by having to pay privately for nursing home long-term care.

Why do most people wind up financially destitute when needing long-term care? Because of the enormous expense.

The average cost of a nursing home in Northern Virginia (where I live and work) is more than $100,000 per year. Some costs are much higher; right across the street from my office is a nursing home whose minimum fee is $12,000 a month. It's a very good nursing home, but it's very expensive.

CHAPTER 3

ARE WILLS THE SOLUTION?

In Chapter 1 we discussed many of the problems of probate—what probate is, why it's such a hassle, and why you hear about the nightmares of probate. In Chapter 2 we discussed many of the problems associated with long-term care. Now let's start looking at the possible solutions—starting with wills.

Is a last will and testament a solution for the problem of probate or the problem of long-term care? The short answer is no. Wills are not the solution for either of these problems. What is a will? A will is a legal document. It gets signed, witnessed, and notarized. It lets you nominate your executor—the one that goes to the court and starts that probate process that we talked about in Chapter 1. If you have minor children, it lets you name a guardian for those minor children. A will is an important legal document, but it has some very serious limitations that most people don't understand.

The biggest drawback of a will is that it puts your estate through the nightmare of probate. That's the sole purpose of a will—it serves as a set of instructions to the probate court, telling the probate court, "here's who I want my assets to go to, here's who I want to be my executor, and here's how I want my estate handled." If you don't have a will when you die, it's called dying "intestate," and your estate will also go through probate. Probate is the exact same process whether you die with a will or without a will; it's just that without a will, your estate will be distributed to your legal heirs, subject to the laws of intestacy. As mentioned in Chapter 1, every state has written a simple will for you. With or without a will, your assets go through the exact same probate process.

Another big problem with the will is that it doesn't control all of your assets. Most people think that when they have a will, it's going to control everything, but it doesn't. We'll talk about why in the next chapter on joint ownership problems.

Another problem with a will is that many people use a will to set up a trust upon their death. It's called a testamentary trust. It takes effect by virtue of the last will and testament. The testamentary trust is simply an extension of probate; and, in many states, such as Virginia, a testamentary trust is going to prolong the probate process. For instance, if you have a testamentary trust that says, "Keep everything in trust for my children until they become age twenty-five" and you have an eleven-year-old child when you die, your estate would be in probate for fourteen years, and your executor would have to file those horrendous annual accountings—the same type we talked about Joan doing in Chapter 1—every year for fourteen years. Talk about a nightmare!

And, of course, a will only goes into effect at death. A will has no effect on your assets while you're alive and certainly does not protect those assets from the expenses of long-term care.

CHAPTER 4

JOINT OWNERSHIP PROBLEMS

Does joint ownership or beneficiary designations help protect assets from probate or long-term care?

Many people attempt to use joint ownership as a sort of inexpensive way to avoid probate. They think they're avoiding probate, and it works sometimes. But what's critical to understand is that joint ownership does not always work as a solution for avoiding probate.

For married couples, you're not avoiding probate, you're just delaying probate until the death of the second spouse. When you start getting into joint ownership between a parent and a child, you often wind up with lots of problems. Here's an example.

CASE STUDY: PROBLEMS WITH JOINT OWNERSHIP

Background
Priscilla came in to see us a few years ago. She was an eighty-two-year-old woman, recently widowed. After her husband

died, Priscilla went into her local bank where she had almost all of their assets and various investments to take her husband's name off of everything. Her oldest daughter, Pam, drove her to the bank because at that point, Priscilla was no longer driving.

The bank executive, trying to be helpful, said to Priscilla, "Because you're taking your husband's name off these accounts, why don't you add your daughter here to the accounts as a joint owner? That way she can write checks for you to pay your bills if there comes a time when you're not able to do that."

Priscilla thought the bank executive surely knew what he was talking about, and so, without legal advice, Priscilla followed his recommendation and added Pam's name as a joint owner on all of Priscilla's accounts.

Sometimes You Can't Trust In-Laws

It was about a year later when Priscilla came to see us, telling us that all of her accounts had judgment liens and tax liens on them. The reason for this was some financial trouble that her daughter had gotten into. Except it wasn't even the daughter; it was the daughter's husband.

What happened is that the daughter's husband, Jack, had started a business a while back. This was a new business, and, of course, Jack had taken out loans to help fund the new venture. When it came time to sign the loan documents, the lender wanted a personal guarantee and the business-owner's spouse to sign, so Pam signed various documents pledging their house and all of their bank and investment accounts as collateral for the loan.

Well, as happens with so many small businesses, Jack's business failed, and the bank, as well as the IRS (which hadn't been paid some overdue taxes), came calling, got liens against Jack and Pam, and because Pam's name was on all of Priscilla's accounts, all of Priscilla's accounts got attached by these judgments and liens. This was the beginning of an unbelievable nightmare.

Sometimes You Can't Trust Bank Officers

The other thing that happened in this case, which Priscilla didn't even realize, is that by adding Pam's name to all of her accounts, she had unintentionally disinherited her other two children. Remember when we said in Chapter 3 that a will doesn't control all of your assets? This is a perfect example. Priscilla had a will that said, "I leave everything in equal shares to my husband, but if my husband has predeceased me, then to my three children in equal shares."

Sounds simple, right? But it's not, because what Priscilla didn't understand (and what most people don't understand) is that joint ownership takes priority over a will. The better way to allow someone to pay your bills and help manage your financial affairs is by using a general power of attorney, not joint ownership.

When we explained this to Priscilla, she was horrified, and she assured us that she would go to her bank as soon as possible and get this fixed by removing Pam's name as a joint owner and instead giving the bank a copy of the power of attorney that we had prepared for Priscilla, wherein she appointed Pam as her agent to pay her bills and help Priscilla manage her financial affairs.

Sadly, while getting her mail a few days later, Priscilla slipped on the ice and broke her hip. She died the next day during her surgery. Priscilla had not made it back to the bank to remove Pam from her accounts.

Sometimes You Can't Trust Siblings

Pam's siblings came to see us a few months after Priscilla's death, having just received the notice to heirs from their sister, Pam. They knew they were named equally with Pam in their mom's will, but Pam had already told them that they wouldn't be receiving any inheritance. According to Pam, their mother "obviously" wanted Pam to inherit everything, because Pam was the one who was providing the most help to Priscilla—

taking her to the doctor's appointments, helping around the house, and helping her pay her bills. That's one of the reasons, according to Pam, that Priscilla added Pam's name to her accounts.

Pam's siblings wanted to know what could be done for them to receive what they considered to be their "rightful share" of the estate. According to them, their mother had told them before she died about her meeting with our firm and how she was going to go to the bank as soon as possible and remove Pam's name from the accounts so that everything would then pass equally to all three kids through her will.

Regretfully, we had to tell Pam's siblings that there was really nothing they could do, as joint ownership prevails over the will. They could have hired another attorney and filed a lawsuit to try to force Pam to disgorge two-thirds of the estate to them, but we told them that such a lawsuit would likely cost tens of thousands of dollars and they would be very unlikely to win.

JOINT OWNERSHIP IS COMPLEX, AND THERE ARE MANY TYPES

Another problem with joint ownership is that the laws of joint ownership are very complex—there are at least four different types of joint ownership, and the laws regarding the meaning and interpretation of these different types of joint ownership vary from state to state. The four most common types of joint ownership are joint tenants with right of survivorship, tenancy by the entirety, community property, and tenancy in common. For some archaic reason, the law still uses the word "tenant" instead of "owner." Here's a general explanation of each type of joint ownership.

Joint Tenants with Rights of Survivorship

This type of ownership, sometimes abbreviated as "JTWROS" or "JTROS," means that if one owner dies, the surviving owner or owners will continue to own the asset.

Tenancy by the Entirety

A special type of joint ownership with right of survivorship that is recognized only between married couples, and only in about eighteen states, often abbreviated as "TBE" or "T/E." And to make it more complicated, in some of the states where it's allowed, it's only for real estate.

Community Property

A special type of joint ownership recognized only between married couples, and only in nine states. And some of these states also recognize a type of joint ownership called quasicommunity property. Worse yet, there are no two community property states with exactly the same laws on the subject.

Tenancy in Common

When property is owned by two or more people as tenants in common (often abbreviated as "TiC" or "T/C"), each owner is deemed to own a percentage of ownership interest in the property. The percentages don't have to be equal. With tenancy in common, when an owner dies, that owner's share does not pass to the other joint owners, so this type of ownership is also called "joint tenants without right of survivorship."

There are two common problems with joint ownership:

1. Many people title bank accounts and other financial accounts in joint names without knowing whether they are taking ownership as joint tenants with right of survivorship or joint tenants without right of survivorship (tenants in common).

2. Deeds to real estate should always be prepared by an attorney; however, many people purchase real estate, or add owners to real estate, by preparing deeds on their own and simply listing two names as owners, or using the term "joint owners" or "co-owners" without specifying whether the ownership is with or without survivorship.

When this is done, the laws of the state in question will determine what happens to that property when one of the owners dies. The laws of some states presume survivorship. The laws of other states presume no survivorship.

A common problem with property owned by two people as joint tenants without survivorship (tenants in common) is that the asset winds up in probate upon the death of the first co-owner. Worse yet, if the share of the deceased co-owner passes to a minor, or to someone who's disabled or incompetent, it winds up stuck in probate for many years and can also cause lots of other problems. Here's an example of the problems with joint ownership.

CASE STUDY: MORE JOINT OWNERSHIP PROBLEMS

In an attempt to avoid probate, Fred, a widower, wanted to add his daughter, Janet, to the deed on his home in Virginia. In an attempt to avoid legal fees, Fred prepared the deed himself, based on a sample deed he found online. The deed transferred the house from Fred alone to Fred and Janet as joint owners.

Fred of course assumed that he would die first and that the property would pass to Janet automatically through right of survivorship. He was wrong on both assumptions.

Janet tragically died from cancer just a few years after Fred added her name to the deed, while Fred was still alive. Instead of Janet's interest passing back to Fred through right of survivorship, Janet's interest passed to her two young twin sons, age seven, because Fred didn't specifically use the words "right of survivorship" in the deed.

Fred didn't even realize that Janet's interest passed to her children until Fred went to sell his house about six months later to move to Florida. Fred (always wanting to save money) put an ad in the paper, stuck a "For Sale by Owner" sign in his front yard, and started to show the house. His house was in great condition, and it didn't take him long to find a buyer. The buyer's attorney prepared and presented the contract to Fred, and Fred signed it. Planning to use all the money from the sale of his Virginia house to purchase his new house, Fred went ahead and signed a contract for a new house in Florida as soon as he had signed the contract to sell his Virginia house. He scheduled the Florida closing for three days after the closing on the Virginia house.

The day before the closing on the sale of the Virginia house, the closing attorney called Fred to tell him that the title examiner had just completed the title search, and he noticed that Janet's name was on the deed. The attorney explained to Fred that Janet would need to be at the closing to sign the deed because she was a co-owner. When Fred told the attorney that Janet had died six months earlier, things started to get very complicated.

The attorney explained to Fred that under state law, Janet's interest passed to her young sons when she died because of the way that Fred had worded the deed. Furthermore, because the children were under eighteen, they could not sign any legal documents; rather, someone would have to go to court to qualify to become the financial guardian for the boys and hold their half of the house, or their half of the sales proceeds, until both children turned eighteen. During those eleven years, the financial guardian would be subject to court-supervised "living" probate—forced to file annual accountings with the probate court until both children turn eighteen. And then, at age eighteen, each child would be entitled to receive his share outright.

Only the financial guardian could sign the closing documents on behalf of the children, so the closing had to be delayed for approximately a month while the father of the boys hired a law firm (that's where we came in) to petition the court to become the boys' financial guardian. During our initial consultation with the boys' father, he told us that one of the twins, Jake, was severely autistic and would probably never be able to live on his own or hold down a job. Based on this fact, we explained that we needed to prepare a specific type of special needs trust (called a First-Party SNT or d4A trust) for the benefit of Jake, and instead of asking to have Jake's share held until age eighteen, we would ask the court to have his share transferred into the new SNT and held in trust for Jake's entire lifetime, in order to protect the assets of the trust from disqualifying Jake from Medicaid and Supplemental Security Income (SSI)—two vital public benefits that he would need as an adult. We explained to Jake's father that this SNT needed to have a "payback provision," providing for any balance remaining in the trust at Jake's death to be paid back to the state to reimburse the state for any Medicaid funds that had been used for Jake during his lifetime. We also explained to Jake's dad that this payback provision could have been avoided had Janet done proper estate planning by setting up a third-party special needs trust for Jake before she died. Although it was too late to do this for Janet, we did do proper estate planning, including a third-party special needs trust, for Jake's dad. (For a more detailed explanation of special needs trusts, please see the section "Special Needs Estate Planning" on page 52.)

The terrible results of Fred's self-guided attempt to avoid probate were staggering:

1. Fred literally lost half of the value in his house. It became owned by Janet's children the moment Janet died. Fred never got any of it back.

2. You'll recall that Fred was going to use all of his sales proceeds from the Virginia home to purchase the new Florida home. But because Fred lost half the value of his Virginia home, he was no longer able to afford to purchase the Florida home. This resulted in the sellers of the Florida home having to sell that home to a new buyer, and for $45,000 less because the real estate market had taken a nosedive in the meantime. They wound up successfully suing Fred for their loss, and Fred was now out another $45,000.

3. Because he was now unable to afford to buy the Florida home, Fred told the buyers of his Virginia home that he was cancelling the contract. But the buyers of his Virginia home were not interested in cancelling the contract; they wanted the house and they had already sold and moved out of their prior home and they had the moving van packed up and were ready to move in. They wound up successfully suing Fred for what's called "specific performance"—forcing him to go through with the sale. They also successfully sued him for all of their monetary damages. Because the closing on the Virginia house had to be delayed for a month, the buyers had to stay in a hotel for a month. They had to pay their moving company for a second complete move, as well as a month of storage fees, because the moving van had to unpack everything into a storage unit and redo the entire move a month later. So, in addition to being forced to sell the property and become homeless, all the delay cost Fred an extra $18,000 in damages he had to pay the buyers.

4. While not directly affecting Fred, the father of Janet's sons was not too happy about having to go to court to become financial guardian, or having to file accountings with the probate court every year for eleven years.

JOINT OWNERSHIP AND DISABILITY

Another problem with joint ownership arises when a joint owner becomes disabled. Disabled persons often receive public benefits—Medicaid to pay health-care expenses and Supplemental Security Income to help pay bills on a monthly basis. When a disabled person gets money from joint ownership or due to a beneficiary designation, he or she can be disqualified from receiving these vital public benefits.

CHAPTER 5

PROBLEMS WITH BENEFICIARY DESIGNATIONS

Most people are familiar with beneficiary designations, and many people attempt to use beneficiary designations as an informal way to avoid probate. But, as I'll explain in this chapter, beneficiary designations do not always solve the problem of probate and can actually cause many more problems than they solve.

WHAT ARE BENEFICIARY DESIGNATIONS?

Some types of assets can be titled with a named beneficiary—someone who is entitled to receive the assets directly after the death of the owner. Insurance policies and retirement plans use the term "beneficiary," but depending on the type of asset involved, a beneficiary designation may be called something different. For example, most banks use the term "POD" (which stands for "pay on death") for bank accounts and Certificates of Deposit. The federal government uses the term POD for savings bonds and other treasury instruments. Securities (stocks, bonds, and brokerage) accounts typically use the term "TOD," which stands for "transfer on death." Regardless of the specific nomenclature used, all beneficiary designations work essentially the same way.

HOW DO BENEFICIARY DESIGNATIONS WORK?

If you're the owner, you retain complete control of your assets while you're alive, and you can change the named beneficiary at any time. After your death, the named beneficiary typically fills out a claim form and files it with the financial institution, along with a death certificate showing proof of your death. Upon acceptance of the claim, the idea is that the financial institution distributes the asset to your named beneficiary. This distribution is typically intended to pass directly to the named beneficiary outside of probate, but, as we'll see, it doesn't always work out the way it's intended.

WHAT ARE THE PROBLEMS WITH BENEFICIARY DESIGNATIONS?

Because of the numerous potential problems with beneficiary designations, my firm doesn't generally recommend them to my clients as a means to avoid probate. The following are types of problems that can be caused by beneficiary designations.

Beneficiary Designations Don't Work for All Types of Assets

Not all assets can be titled with a beneficiary designation. In most states, cars and real estate cannot be owned with a beneficiary designation. Many financial institutions don't offer POD or TOD accounts. Tangible personal property—i.e., home furnishings, jewelry, etc.—is not generally capable of being titled with a beneficiary designation, because such items do not generally have any documents of title establishing ownership. Because not all assets can be titled with a beneficiary designation, if you try to avoid probate by using beneficiary designations, some assets will typically still have to go through probate.

Beneficiary Designations Are Tedious to Change

There is no single document where you can simply list your assets and declare them "payable on death." To establish a beneficiary designation for each asset, you must fill out a separate beneficiary designation form at the financial institution holding each asset. Every asset that you wish to make "payable on death" has to be individually changed. If you later wish to change your beneficiary designations, you must change each one individually all over again.

Beneficiary Designations Don't Work for Minors

Beneficiary designations should never intentionally be used as a way to distribute assets to minors, because children under the age of eighteen are not legally allowed to control assets. If a minor does inherit assets, those assets will have to be held in a court-supervised "living probate"—identical to the probate process described in Chapter 1—requiring detailed record keeping, annual accountings, and all the other complications, hassles, and expenses of probate.

Beneficiary Designations May Not Work If a Beneficiary Predeceases You

If a named beneficiary dies before you, that beneficiary's share will typically "lapse," meaning that the share of that beneficiary will go to your estate, and therefore through probate, where it will eventually be distributed under the terms of your will (if you have one) or under the laws of intestacy for your state of residence.

Beneficiary Designations Don't Work for Disabled Beneficiaries

Beneficiary designations should almost never be used as a way to distribute assets to disabled beneficiaries, for several reasons. First, the inheritance will wind up getting stuck in probate if the disabled beneficiary has been adjudicated to be legally incapacitated and therefore unable to manage assets. Worse, a direct inheritance may disqualify a disabled beneficiary from receiving certain vital public benefits, such as Medicaid and SSI. The proper method for taking care of a beneficiary who is disabled is through a special needs trust, as explained in greater detail in Chapter 7.

CHAPTER 6

ESTATE AND INCAPACITY PLANNING

We all know that we will eventually die. At the same time, no one likes to dwell on the prospect of his or her own death. But like everything else in life, failure to plan means planning to fail. If you, your parents, or other loved ones postpone planning until it is too late, you run the risk that your children or other intended beneficiaries—those you love the most—may not receive all that you would hope, or may not be taken care of in the way you would hope.

That is what estate planning is all about—making sure that your loved ones are taken care of when you are gone. All adults need to do estate planning—whether you have $50,000 or $5 million, you probably want to distribute your assets in a certain way upon your death, which means you need to do estate planning. However, the best estate plan in the world is meaningless if all of your assets wind up being spent on nursing home care before your death, which is why the information in this chapter must be read and understood in light of all the information contained elsewhere in this book.

WHAT IS AN ESTATE?

We should begin a discussion of estate planning with a review of what "estate" and "estate plan" mean. An "estate" is everything you own: bank accounts, stocks and bonds, real estate, motor vehicles, retirement plans, life insurance, jewelry, household furniture, etc. An "estate plan," generally, refers to the means by which your estate is passed on to your loved ones upon your death. Estate planning can be accomplished through a variety of methods, including:

- Revocable Living Trusts
- Last Will and Testament/Probate
- Lifetime Gifting
- Joint Ownership
- Beneficiary Designations
- Life Estates

Problems often arise when people don't have a coordinated method of passing on their estate. To take just one example, a father's will may say that everything should be equally divided among his children, but if the father creates a joint account with only one of the children, there could be a fight about whether the contents of that account should be put back in the pool with the rest of the property or simply go to the child whose name is on the account.

THE TWO TYPES OF PROBATE

Without proper incapacity planning documents, your estate will go into living probate if you become incapacitated while you are alive. Dying without a trust, or using a last will and testament as your primary estate planning tool (or dying without a last will and testament), means that your estate will go through postmortem probate upon your death.

The probate process in most states (both for living probate and postmortem probate) is an unnecessarily complicated, time-consuming, and expensive process that can go on for many years.

If you become incapacitated while you are alive and you don't have proper incapacity planning documents, then someone will have to go to court to have you declared incompetent. This person will seek to become your legal and financial guardian (sometimes the financial guardian is called a conservator).

To initiate the postmortem probate process in most states, an executor nominated in a last will and testament must take the original will and an original death certificate and make at least one appearance at the probate office to officially "qualify" and be "sworn in" as executor. If you died without a will or trust, then someone on your behalf goes to the probate office to become the administrator of your estate. Both an executor of a will and an administrator of an estate are called "personal representatives" and serve the exact same function.

Once officially appointed, a guardian/conservator under a living probate or a personal representative under a postmortem probate is accountable to the probate court and is required to prepare and file various legal and financial documents, usually including an initial inventory of the estate and detailed annual accountings showing everything coming into and going out of the estate. Both a guardian/conservator and a personal representative must see to it that all assets are accounted for and that any valid debts, expenses, and taxes are paid.

Living probate continues for the lifetime of the incapacitated individual. With postmortem probate, typically after a certain period of time from the date of death, the personal representative may distribute the remaining assets of the estate.

INCAPACITY PLANNING

To avoid living probate, you need to have incapacity planning documents in place. Incapacity planning (which can be done by itself or in connection with your estate planning) involves the signing of three important documents: (1) a durable general power of attorney for legal and financial affairs; (2) an advance medical directive, which includes a medical power of attorney, long-term care directive, living will, and postmortem directive;

and (3) a lifestyle care plan. Taken together, these three important documents allow you to decide in advance who will manage your legal, personal, and financial affairs in the event of your disability, and exactly how you will be cared for.

Financial Power of Attorney

Just as a living trust avoids postmortem probate, a durable general financial power of attorney avoids lifetime probate by authorizing your agent to act on your behalf and sign your name to financial and/or legal documents. The financial power of attorney is an essential tool if you are unable to carry on your legal and financial affairs due to age, illness, or injury. Having a financial power of attorney will generally avoid the need to go through the time-consuming, expensive, and publicly embarrassing guardianship and conservatorship process, which process is subject to probate court supervision. During the guardianship and conservatorship process, someone goes to court to have you declared mentally or physically incompetent, and the court appoints one or more persons to serve as your legal guardian and/or conservator—this is the process of living probate.

Power of attorney and guardianship perform similar functions. However, they are vastly different in terms of how someone is appointed, who does the appointing, and how much control the appointed agent or guardian has.

Guardianship is a legal relationship in which the court authorizes one person with the power to make personal and/or financial decisions for another person. The person authorized with decision-making power is known as the guardian, and the person for whom the decisions are being made is known as the ward. Guardianship over the person typically goes along with conservatorship over property, which in some states is called guardianship over property.

Guardianship and conservatorship are assigned when a person has been determined to lack the capacity to make rational and intelligent decisions on their own in regard to their medical decisions and/or finances. Usually it is a family member who applies for guardianship and conservatorship, but it can also be a friend, or in some cases the county or city in which the ward resided. In some cases, a third party may be appointed as guardian and/or conservator, particularly in the case of finances, if no one close to the ward is deemed appropriate.

Conservators are subject to the nightmare of living probate, meaning that, among other things, they must file annual accountings every year with the probate court or commissioner of accounts.

A power of attorney is a legal document that you create to give another person, known as your agent, legal power to act on your behalf. The document can grant either broad and unlimited powers or limited powers to act in specific circumstances or over specific types of decisions.

Typically, a power of attorney is effective immediately, but is intended to be used only when necessary at some future date.

In most cases, power of attorney is greatly preferred to guardianship because:

- Unlike a power of attorney, a guardianship cannot be created voluntarily—it must be granted by a judge.
- You retain control over who makes the decisions and what decisions they can make.
- A power of attorney is significantly less expensive to create compared to applying for guardianship.
- No court is involved when you sign a power of attorney.
- No annual accountings are required to be filed by your agent under your power of attorney, although in most states someone with a legal interest in your financial affairs may request an accounting from your agent.
- A power of attorney offers privacy, whereas guardianship and conservatorship probate court proceedings are public records.

- You may revoke the power of attorney at any time so long as you have the mental capacity to do so, whereas a guardianship and conservatorship can only be revoked by the court that granted it in the first place.

Advance Medical Directive

An advance medical directive (also called a health-care power of attorney, or medical power of attorney, or health-care proxy) authorizes another person (called your "medical agent") to make decisions with respect to your medical care in the event that you are physically or mentally unable to do so, as certified by two physicians. The advance medical directive that we use in our firm is a proprietary document called the Four Needs Advance Directive™—this document includes four major sections:

1. A **medical power of attorney** names someone to make health-care decisions for you while you are in a hospital, and someone to give informed consent on your behalf, if you are no longer able.
2. A **long-term care directive** allows you to make long-term care decisions for yourself in case you wind up in a nursing home.
3. The **near-death directive** (sometimes called a living will) part of the document deals with end-of-life decision-making and allows you to indicate your wishes concerning the use of artificial or extraordinary measures to prolong your life artificially in the event of a terminal illness or injury.
4. The **postmortem directive** covers issues such as disposition of bodily remains, organ donation, and funeral arrangements.

Lifestyle Care Plan

A lifestyle care plan is a document that is created by special software that gathers, organizes, stores, and disseminates information provided by you in an interview, in order to better serve your future health-care needs and to guide those who you will depend on for future care. The lifestyle care plan identifies your specific needs, desires, habits, and preferences and guides your caregiver in a unique manner. See the following chart on incapacity planning for a detailed example of the tremendous benefits of a lifestyle care plan.

The following example of a lifestyle care plan is provided by Advance Care Planning, Inc., and it shows how the plan can help improve a day in the life of Lynn, a typical nursing home resident.

Lynn, at the age of eighty-five, has been placed in the nursing home due to a stroke. She is incontinent, but if taken to the restroom at appropriate times, she will be continent most of the time. She is alert, but somewhat confused at times. She very much knows what she wants but cannot always verbalize it. She is able to feed herself finger foods.

Without a Lifestyle Care Plan	With a Lifestyle Care Plan
5:30 a.m.: Awakened. Hospital gown taken off, given some quick care, dressed for the day in someone else's house dress. It is a pretty house dress, but she does not like house dresses.	*7:00 a.m.*: Awakened. Taken to the bathroom for quick morning care, then placed in a comfortable chair in her room in front of the TV with a requested show on to await breakfast. Stays in her short PJs and a robe, since it is a shower day.
7:30 a.m.: Taken to the dining room for breakfast. Given one cup of coffee, not offered more coffee. Not served bacon due to her high cholesterol.	*7:30 a.m.*: Served bacon and eggs for breakfast. Her cholesterol is high, but she stated her wishes to eat a regular diet, including bacon and eggs for breakfast, in her Lifestyle Care Plan. She has two cups of coffee, as she has done for the last 65 years.

After Breakfast: Taken to sit in the hallway outside of her room.	*After Breakfast*: Taken to the bathroom and then to shower room. Her hair is washed, as it is with every shower per her Lifestyle Care Plan. She prefers to shower in the morning. After shower, dressed in her navy blue jogging suit with her red tee shirt, per her Lifestyle Care Plan.
1–2 Hours Later: Taken to her room, has her brief changed, and then is set in the hallway by the nurse's station. Her lips were not moistened, nor does she have access to lip moisturizer.	*1–2 Hours Later*: Has her lip moisturizer around her neck and is able to put it on herself frequently. Though her lips do not look dry, they feel dry to her. Her Lifestyle Care Plan notes that the staff should help her moisten her lips frequently.
10:00 a.m.: Given six pills— two for high cholesterol, one for irregular heartbeat, one for hiatal hernia to prevent heartburn, one for hypertension, and one for arthritis.	*10:00 a.m.*: Given three pills—one for hiatal hernia to prevent heartburn, one for hypertension, and one for arthritis. Decided in her Lifestyle Care Plan that if she ever entered a nursing home, she would prefer not to take the other medications.
11:00 a.m.: Still sitting in the hall by the nurse's station.	*11:00 a.m.*: Taken outside to sit in the shade. She does not like crafts but prefers to be outside in the shade, weather permitting.

12:00 Noon: Taken to the dining room for lunch. Given a lean hamburger, no salt allowed, a salad with low-fat dressing, and applesauce. Needs assistance with the applesauce.	*12:00 Noon*: Taken back to her room for lunch; placed in her chair in front of the TV with her program of choice. Given a cheeseburger, packets of salt, french fries, and apple slices. Her Lifestyle Care Plan states that she does not want to be spoon-fed and would prefer finger foods.
After Lunch: Taken to the nurse's station to sit in the hallway.	*After Lunch*: Taken to the restroom and then placed in her recliner to rest and watch her favorite movie on her DVD player.
2:00 p.m.: Placed in bed to have brief changed, and to rest.	*2:00 p.m.*: Still watching her movie.
3:30 p.m.: Placed in wheelchair and taken to ceramics class.	*3:30 p.m.*: Gets her weekly manicure instead of going to ceramics class. She does not like crafts.
5:00 p.m.: Taken to room to have brief changed.	*5:00 p.m.*: Taken to the restroom. Prepared for dinner.
5:30 p.m.: Taken to dining room for dinner. Served chicken. Lynn loves hot dogs, but they are not served to her due to her high cholesterol.	*5:30 p.m.*: Placed in her chair in her room for dinner. Served hot dogs with green pepper slices, cherry tomatoes, and veggie dip. Enjoyed a brownie for dessert.

After Dinner: Taken to the nurse's station to sit in the hall. There is a TV with DVD at the nurse's station; staff puts a movie on for those sitting in the hall to watch. The movie is one that Lynn has seen several times and does not like.	*After Dinner*: She continues to watch TV until 7:30 p.m.
8:30 p.m.: Taken to the shower. She prefers to bathe in the morning.	*7:30 p.m.*: Taken to the bathroom and helped to prepare for bed. She wears her short pajamas per her Lifestyle Care Plan.
After Shower: Dressed in a hospital gown and put to bed with one pillow at her head.	*8:00 p.m.*: Placed in bed with an audio book. It is a legal mystery, the type of book she likes. She has stated in her Lifestyle Care Plan that she likes to go to bed by 8:00 p.m. to read. She is only able to make use of audio books at this time.
The room is 75 degrees, and she is very warm. She throws her covers off since she is too warm to sleep. The staff does come in and turn her several times. They place her on her back (she has never been able to sleep on her back), and they always cover her back up. Her brief is changed once during the night.	In bed, she has down pillows (5 ft.) on either side of her, between her legs, and 3 at her head, as she has slept for 40 years. The room temperature is 70 degrees, which is slightly warm for her. The temperature cannot be adjusted due to her roommate, so her personal fan is turned on to keep her cooler. She sleeps well but is awakened by the staff twice to take her to the toilet, per her Lifestyle Care Plan. She remains continent at night.

The following day, she falls asleep in her chair by the nurse's station, since she did not sleep well the night before. Her children come to take her out to lunch but she appears too sleepy, so she does not go.	The following day she is rested and has a strong sense of well-being. Her children come and take her to lunch. She is gone several hours and rests in her chair for two hours upon her return.

ESTATE PLANNING

A well-crafted estate plan could permit your family to save potentially tens or even hundreds of thousands of dollars on taxes, court costs, and attorneys' fees. Most important, it affords the comfort that your loved ones can mourn your loss without being simultaneously burdened with unnecessary red tape and financial confusion.

Estate planning (including the decision as to whether to use a will or a living trust as your primary estate planning tool) is vitally important for someone who may soon be entering a nursing home.

Just as a good incapacity plan avoids lifetime probate, a good estate plan—one that uses a revocable living trust as the primary estate planning tool—avoids postmortem probate.

REVOCABLE LIVING TRUSTS

A trust is a legal entity that is capable of owning financial assets, real estate, and/or other property.

A living trust is a trust that comes into existence during your lifetime, and a revocable living trust is simply a living trust that can be revoked or modified during your lifetime, as opposed to some living trusts that are irrevocable. Using a fully funded revocable living trust as your primary estate planning tool means that your estate will not go through probate after your death. You create a revocable living trust by signing a contractual document called a "declaration of trust" or "trust agreement."

You are typically the trustee of your own living trust until your death. If you are the initial trustee, then upon your death or disability, a successor trustee whom you have named takes over as trustee of the trust and, after paying any valid debts, expenses, and taxes, distributes the trust assets to or for the benefit of your named beneficiaries or, if called for in the trust, continues to hold the trust assets until the occurrence of a predetermined event.

The main feature of a revocable living trust is that the trustee is not accountable to the court, and therefore not subject to probate. Therefore, most people use a revocable living trust as their primary estate planning tool in order to make things easier for their trusted loved ones by avoiding the time and complications of probate. There are also some advantages of using a revocable living trust to consolidate your assets and simplify your finances while you're alive.

What Are the Benefits of a Revocable Living Trust?

A will puts your estate through the nightmare of probate when you die. Fortunately, the revocable living trust is a simple and proven alternative to a will that avoids probate and lets you keep control of your assets while you're alive and distributes your assets according to your wishes upon your death.

What Is a Revocable Living Trust?

A revocable living trust is an entity, created by a legal document that, like a will, contains your instructions for what you want to happen to your assets when you die. Assets in your revocable living trust avoid probate at death because a trust does not die. A revocable living trust does not protect your assets from lawsuits or nursing home expenses.

How Does a Living Trust Avoid Probate?

When you establish a revocable living trust, you retitle your assets from your name to the name of your trust, which you control as trustee. For example, we will prepare a deed that transfers the house from "John and Mary Doe" to "John and Mary Doe, Trustees under the John and Mary Doe Trust." The goal is for you to legally no longer own anything. If, upon your death, everything belongs to your trust, there is nothing to go through probate.

Do I Lose Control of the Assets in My Revocable Living Trust?

No. You keep full control. As trustee of your revocable living trust, you can do anything you could do before—buy and sell assets, change investments, and even revoke your trust.

Do I Have to File a Separate Tax Return for My Revocable Living Trust?

No. You file the same IRS 1040 tax return that you always have. A revocable living trust requires no extra tax filings.

Is It Hard to Transfer Assets into My Trust?

No. The process is called "trust funding." Your lawyer will take care of retitling all real estate. If you have a financial advisor and/or insurance agent, they can help with trust funding. Alternatively, simply call each of your financial institutions and tell them you're creating a trust, and ask each one to send you the proper form to fill out (every financial institution has its own form). Be sure to not delay funding your revocable living trust, as your revocable living trust can only protect assets that have been retitled into it. Beneficiary designations (for example, with insurance policies and IRAs) should also typically be changed to your trust so the court can't control them if a beneficiary is incapacitated or no longer living when you die.

Is Funding the Trust Time Consuming?

It will take some extra effort and time to fund your trust as opposed to just doing a will, but you can either take this extra time now, or your estate can pay the courts and attorneys to guide your estate through the nightmare of probate for you upon your death. If you want to make things easier for your family upon your death, a trust is absolutely the way to go. A will may be slightly easier for you now, but it creates a nightmare for your family upon your death.

Who Controls the Trust Assets While I'm Alive?

The trustee manages all of the assets inside the trust. If you're not married, you will typically be the sole trustee of your trust and have full use of and control over all trust assets. If you're married and don't have children from a prior relationship, then typically you will have a joint trust and you and your spouse will be co-trustees, meaning both of you have full use of and control over all trust assets and, if one of you becomes incapacitated or dies, the other spouse simply continues to act as the sole trustee of the trust. If you are married, but one or both of you have children from a prior relationship, then you will often have two separate trusts, with each of you controlling your own trust. If something happens to the initial trustee(s) of a trust, then a successor trustee whom you have selected will step in and take over managing the trust assets.

Who Controls the Truth Assets after My Death?

Upon your death, or if you become incapacitated, the successor trustee or co-trustees whom you named in the trust document take over managing the assets in the trust. When you die, your successor trustee pays your debts, files your tax returns, and distributes your assets. All of this can be done quickly and privately, according to the instructions spelled out in your trust, without any court involvement.

Who Can Be Successor Trustees?

Successor trustees are typically individuals, such as your adult children, other relatives, or trusted friends. Alternatively, you can name a professional trustee such as a trust company or law firm. If you choose an individual, you should also name additional successors in case your first choice is unable or unwilling to act as your trustee.

Does My Trust End When I Die?

Unlike a will, a trust does not die when you die. Assets can stay in your trust as long as you want them to, and be managed by the successor trustee(s) you selected, until your beneficiaries reach the age(s) you want them to inherit. Your trust can even continue for a loved one's lifetime if you have a beneficiary with special needs, or to protect the assets from a beneficiary's future possible creditors, such as a lawsuit, a divorce, or catastrophic medical or nursing home expenses.

Can't a Trust Inside a Will Do the Same Thing?

Yes, but with a huge downside. A will can contain wording to create what's called a "testamentary trust" after your death. But because the testamentary trust is part of your will, a testamentary trust is an extension of probate, and in Virginia and many other states, the trustee of a testamentary trust has to file annual accountings with the court every year that the testamentary trust remains in existence. So, for example, the trustee of a testamentary trust for a minor will have to file accountings with the court every year until the child reaches age eighteen or some other age specified in the will. Even worse, if you have a special needs child, the trustee of your child's testamentary special needs trust will have to file annual accountings for the remainder of your child's lifetime. One of the main reasons for a revocable living trust is to avoid the filing of these horrendous annual accountings.

Is a Revocable Living Trust Expensive?

Although you might save a small amount of money up front by doing a will-based plan instead of a trust-based plan, this small savings is meaningless when compared to all of the costs associated with probate and the nightmare of probate. In the long run, a properly drafted estate plan based around a revocable living trust will save the average estate tens of thousands of dollars or more and will save your loved ones years of frustration and aggravation.

Does It Take Longer to Get a Revocable Living Trust?

With most attorneys, it takes the same amount of time to draft a will-based plan as it does for a trust-based plan.

Should I Have an Attorney Prepare My Trust?

Of course, but it's very important to hire the right attorney. Find one with at least twenty years of experience to give you the peace of mind that your trust is prepared and funded properly.

If I Have a Revocable Living Trust, Do I Still Need a Will?

Yes, you need a "pour-over" will that acts as a safety net if you forget to retitle an asset into trust. When you die, the will "catches" the forgotten asset and pours it into your trust. The asset may have to go through probate first, but it can then be distributed as part of your overall living trust plan. If you have children who are minors, you also need a will to appoint guardians.

Are Revocable Living Trusts New?

No. Trusts have been used successfully for hundreds of years, longer than wills have been used.

Who Should Have a Living Trust?

If you own titled assets and want your loved ones to avoid the nightmare of probate upon your death, you should have a revocable living trust to avoid probate. However, if you're over 65 or worried about the future expenses of nursing home care or other long-term care, you should consider my company's Living Trust Plus™ asset protection trust, designed to protect your assets from the nightmare and expenses of probate *plus* lawsuits *plus* nursing home expenses and other long-term care expenses.

CHAPTER 7

SPECIAL NEEDS PLANNING

The primary goal of special needs planning is to protect the quality of life of the person with special needs.

Special needs planning means legal and financial planning that is done for the benefit of a person with special needs. The primary goal of special needs planning is to protect the quality of life of the person with special needs. Money that is legally protected through proper special needs planning can be used to provide a person with special needs enhanced care and a better quality of life while still receiving vital public benefits such as SSI and Medicaid.

Special needs planning is done in a multitude of situations, including estate planning by parents with a special needs child, an individual with special needs coming into an inheritance or settling a personal injury claim, or a spouse planning for a disabled spouse.

This chapter will provide a brief introduction and overview of the different types of special needs planning to assist parents and other relatives of persons with special needs.

SPECIAL NEEDS ESTATE PLANNING

Parents of children with special needs face unique estate planning concerns:

- How do you leave funds for your child without causing the child to lose vital public benefits?
- How do you ensure that the funds are well managed?
- How do you ensure that your other children are not overburdened with caring for their sibling?
- What is a fair way to divide your estate?
- How do you ensure there's enough money to meet your disabled child's needs?

Parents of special needs children often try to resolve these concerns by leaving the special needs child's share to a healthy child, disinheriting the child with special needs. Parents who choose this approach may have been told, incorrectly, that their special needs child can't inherit anything because he will lose his public benefits. Parents may also mistakenly think that their child won't need an inheritance because he'll be taken care of by public benefits. This type of planning also assumes that the healthy child will in fact use the money to take care of the special needs sibling.

The approach of disinheriting your special needs child is generally discouraged for a number of reasons. First, public benefits programs are often inadequate to provide complete support and assistance for a person with special needs. Public benefits need to be supplemented with other resources in order to provide optimal care. Second, both public benefits programs and individual circumstances change over time; what's working today may not work tomorrow, so other resources need to be available. Third, relying on a healthy child to take care of a special needs sibling may place an undue burden on the healthy child and can strain relations between them. It makes it unclear whether inherited money belongs to the healthy child to spend as he or she pleases, or whether it must be set aside for the special needs sibling. When money is used by a healthy child to take care of a special needs sibling, this may trigger gift consequences and create tax and public benefit concerns. Also, if the healthy child gets sued, goes through a messy divorce, or files for bankruptcy, all of the money that was set aside for the special needs child could be lost.

The better solution to all of these problems is a special type of trust called a "special needs trust." Such trusts, also called "supplemental needs trusts," fulfill two primary functions: The first is to manage funds for someone who may not be able to do so himself or herself due to disability. The second is to preserve the beneficiary's eligibility for public benefits, whether that be Medicaid, Supplemental Security Income, public housing, or any other program.

WHAT IS A SPECIAL NEEDS TRUST (SNT)?

First, a short explanation of what trusts are and how they work: a trust is a form of ownership of property, whether real estate or investments, where one person (the trustee) manages such property for the benefit of someone else (the beneficiary). The trustee must follow the instructions laid out in the trust agreement as to how to spend the trust funds on the beneficiary's behalf—whether and when to distribute the trust income and principal. In the special needs context, trusts fall generally into two main categories: third-party SNTs that one person creates and funds for the benefit of someone else, and first-party SNTs that are created for the person with special needs using that person's own money.

THIRD-PARTY SPECIAL NEEDS TRUSTS

A trust that is created and funded by someone for the benefit of a person with special needs is often called a "third party SNT." This type of trust can be created while you are alive by using a revocable or irrevocable living trust, or it can be created upon your death through your living trust or through your will. If you create and fund a third-party SNT during your lifetime, you can place assets into the SNT while you are alive and/or upon your death. This type of third-party SNT can also be used to receive any inheritance that may come from a grandparent or other family member, provided the other family member properly names the SNT that you created. Because the SNT will own the assets, the beneficiary will not become ineligible for government benefits. On the contrary, the SNT allows the beneficiary to receive vital public benefits, while the funds in the SNT can be used for the special needs beneficiary to improve care and quality of life until his or her own death, at which time any assets left in trust can pass to whomever you name in the trust document.

To determine the exact provisions to include in an SNT, a parent should work with a qualified elder law and special needs planning attorney. Your attorney will consider information about you and your disabled beneficiary and how you want the trust funds used. Your attorney will base his or her recommendation on your beneficiary's age, what benefits your beneficiary is receiving or is likely to receive in the future, the eligibility requirements for benefits, and the type and amount of assets you plan to place in the trust.

FIRST-PARTY SPECIAL NEEDS TRUSTS

The previous discussion involves estate planning by parents for money they plan to leave their child with special needs. However, a third-party special needs trust cannot hold funds belonging to the disabled individual himself. Unexpected events may trigger money being paid directly to a person with special needs. This may happen, for example, through an inheritance from a family member, life insurance proceeds, or a personal injury settlement. If a person is about to receive money or property in an amount that will cause him or her to lose benefits, a first-party SNT—often called a "(d)(4)(A)" trust, so named after the US Code section that authorizes this type of trust—is a planning option that can help set aside some or all of the money for supplemental needs and still allow the person to stay on public benefits without any period of disqualification. If a person has already received money or property in an amount that has caused him or her loss of benefits, the first-party SNT can still be used as a tool to set aside some or all of the money for supplemental needs and allow the person to reobtain public benefits.

A (d)(4)(A) trust must be created while the disabled individual is under age sixty-five and can be established by the disabled individual, his or her parent, grandparent, legal guardian, or by a court. A (d)(4)(A) trust also must provide that at the beneficiary's death, any remaining trust funds will first be used to reimburse the state for Medicaid paid on the beneficiary's behalf. Because of this payback provision, this type of trust is sometimes called a "payback trust." The state must approve all payback trusts to make sure that they meet the standards in the law. After the state is paid back, any assets left in the trust can pass to the people chosen by the grantor and named in the trust instrument.

CHOOSING THE SPECIAL NEEDS TRUSTEE

Choosing a trustee is one of the most difficult parts of planning for a person with special needs. The trustee of a special needs trust must be able to fulfill all of the normal functions of a trustee—accounting, investments, tax returns, and distributions—and also be able to meet the needs of the special beneficiary. The latter often means having an understanding of the various public benefits programs, having sensitivity to the needs of the beneficiary, and having knowledge of special services that may be available. There are a number of possible solutions, including professional trustees such as banks, trust companies, and law firms who work with special needs trusts. Often, parents choose to appoint co-trustees—for example, a trust company or law firm as a professional trustee along with a healthy child as a family trustee. Working together, the co-trustees can provide the necessary experience to meet the needs of the child with special needs. Unfortunately, in many cases, such a combination is not available. Some professional trustees require a minimum amount of funds in the trust. In other situations, there is no appropriate family member to appoint as a co-trustee.

Where the size of the trust is insufficient to justify hiring a professional trustee, two other solutions are possible. The first option is simply to have a family member trustee who would hire accountants, attorneys, and investment advisors to help with administering the trust. Where no appropriate family member is available to serve as co-trustee, the parent may direct the professional trustee to consult with specific individuals who know and can care for the child with special needs. These could be family members who are not appropriate trustees, but who can serve in an advisory role. Or they may be social workers or care managers or others who have both personal and professional knowledge of the beneficiary. This role may be formalized in the trust document as a "Care Committee" or "Advisory Committee." The second option is to use a pooled trust.

WHEN TO USE POOLED SPECIAL NEEDS TRUSTS

A pooled SNT is a special type of SNT that is created by a nonprofit organization. The nonprofit organization may act as the trustee of the pooled SNT, or it may select the trustee. Individuals have separate accounts in the pooled SNT, but all the money is pooled together and invested by the trustee. Individual beneficiaries get the services of a professional trustee and more investment options because there is more money overall. A third-party pooled trust provides a way to benefit from a special needs trust without having to create one yourself.

Just as there are third-party and first-party SNTs that are typically created for a single disabled beneficiary, there are both third-party pooled SNTs and first-party pooled SNTs—also called "(d)(4)(C)" trusts. Parents typically use a third-party pooled SNT to leave assets upon death of the parents for their special needs child. A first-party pooled SNT is used to protect money that already belongs to the special needs beneficiary. Unlike the (d)(4)(A) discussed previously, at the beneficiary's death, the state does not have to be repaid for Medicaid expenses as long as the funds are retained in the trust for the benefit of other disabled beneficiaries. Although a pooled trust is an option for a disabled individual over age sixty-five who is receiving Medicaid or SSI, those over age sixty-five who make transfers to this type of trust may incur a transfer penalty.

FUNDING THE THIRD-PARTY SPECIAL NEEDS TRUST

As a parent or guardian, you want to ensure that your child with special needs will remain financially secure even when you are no longer there to provide support. Given the significant, ongoing expenses involved in your child's care and uncertainty about what needs may arise after you are gone or what public benefits may be available, determining how much a special needs trust (SNT) should hold is no small feat.

Fortunately, help in calculating your "special needs goal" is available from financial planners with expertise in disability issues, as well as from special needs calculators, which are accessible free of charge on the Internet from sites such as: **Merrill Lynch Special Needs Calculator:** http://specialneedscalc.ml.com.

Using one of these calculators, either on your own or with the help of an advisor, is an excellent way to begin making concrete plans for your child's future. Based on information you provide about anticipated income and expenses, the calculators offer a realistic estimate of how much your child will need in lifetime financial support. Financial planners suggest running this type of calculation periodically, particularly as your child nears adulthood, to ensure the estimate reflects the most accurate, up-to-date information about needs and circumstances.

Getting Started with Funding

The first step in determining the amount you must set aside in an SNT is to consider your goals and your expectations for your child's future. If you haven't yet created a "letter of intent" or an "advance care plan" for your child, this is the time to draft such a document. The letter of intent or advance care plan should address factors such as your child's medical condition, guardianship needs, ability to work, and desired living arrangements, all of which will drive your special needs calculation.

Once you've considered the "big picture," you'll need to identify your child's future income sources and living expenses. The online calculators identify relevant categories for you (e.g., public benefits income and transportation costs).

Next, you'll need to tackle the most arduous part of the process, which is placing a dollar value on each category. You can start by listing any current income or expenses likely to continue into your child's adult years. You'll need to consider income from sources such as life insurance proceeds, gifts, inheritances, and legal settlements, as well as from employment and public benefits such as Supplemental Security Income and Social Security Disability Income.

On the expenses side of the column, broad categories include, but are not necessarily limited to, the following:

- Housing: rent, a mortgage, utilities, insurance, taxes, maintenance
- Transportation: car payments, auto insurance, fuel, repairs, public transportation costs
- Medical care: doctor visits, therapy, prescription drugs
- Care assistance: respite, custodial, nursing home care
- Special equipment: wheelchairs, assistive technologies, durable medical equipment, computers, service animals
- Personal needs: grooming, hobbies, entertainment, vacations

- Education and employment costs: tuition, books, supplies, tutoring
- Future asset replacement costs: for a car, major appliances, electronics, furnishings

Running the Funding Calculation

Prior to running the calculation, you may need to indicate your child's life expectancy and the number of years remaining until your retirement. Once you've input all required data, the calculator will run an analysis of your funding needs based on preset assumptions about the rate of inflation and your after-tax investment returns. The calculator listed on page 57 indicates the amount of annual savings required to meet your goal. The Merrill Lynch calculation includes a lump-sum savings goal that must be met by retirement, as well as a year-by-year cash-flow analysis indicating any shortfalls or surpluses for a given year.

Considering the Funding "What Ifs"

Financial planners advise that running alternative calculations can help you plan adequately for worst- and best-case scenarios. One variable to consider is your child's ability to earn income. For example, if he or she is able to work more than expected, earned income may cover more expenses, but SSI payments will likely be reduced. As your child's disability advances, he or she may need to leave the workforce, potentially increasing SSI payments but also adding new expenses.

Another critical factor is the impact of higher or lower investment returns on the amount you set aside. If your child is very young, you may plan to invest aggressively, pursuing a higher rate of return than if he or she were nearing adulthood. An investment "rule of thumb" is that you generally can take somewhat greater risks with a longer-term investment because you have more time to recover from dips in the market. If you anticipate a lower rate of return for any reason, you will need to compensate by setting aside more in savings.

As you can see, to some extent, this is more of an art than a science. You can make your best guess or work with a financial planner who specializes in this field and who can bring to bear his or her experience with many families in similar situations.

Finding the Funds—Using Life Insurance

Once you have a realistic estimate in hand, you'll need to consider how to fund this need without sacrificing such financial goals as college for your other children and retirement for yourselves. You also need to balance the needs of your special needs child with your wish to benefit your other children, as well as cover your current expenses. You may not be able to completely fund the dollar amount resulting from the calculations, but having a target can assist your planning.

Many parents find that a second-to-die life insurance policy is the easiest option to fund an SNT because the premiums are often lower. However, a joint first-to-die policy might make more sense for many parents, especially if one parent is the primary wage earner and one parent is the primary caregiver for the disabled child. With a first-to-die policy, if the wage-earner parent dies first, the policy will provide funds needed for the caregiver parent to be able to continue providing the care; if the caregiver parent dies first, the policy will provide funds needed for the wage-earner parent to hire a replacement caregiver.

Conclusion about Funding an SNT

In short, how much you fund your SNT and how large an insurance policy you purchase will be a question of balance among your current needs, your retirement funding, the needs of your other children, if any, and the anticipated needs of your special needs child.

Finally, be sure to create or update your estate plan and determine which of your assets you'll leave to the SNT. To avoid the risk of disqualifying the child from eligibility for public benefits, also advise relatives of the need to direct gifts and bequests to the SNT, rather than to the child.

CHAPTER 8

WHAT IS A NURSING HOME?

Nursing homes have only been around since the 1950s, but most likely you, or someone close to you, have spent time in a nursing home. Over the past several decades, nursing homes have become big business. The vast majority of all nursing homes are for-profit entities, and many of these are large corporations with nursing facilities in multiple states. Nursing homes generally provide three types of services:

1. Rehabilitation for people who are injured, sick, or disabled
2. Skilled nursing and medical care
3. Custodial care (help with eating, dressing, bathing, toileting, and moving about)

Like hospitals, nursing homes never close—service must be available twenty-four hours a day, 365 days a year with trained, licensed nursing staff always present. A nursing facility is required to maintain interdisciplinary staffing at several levels, including licensed nursing facility administrators and physician medical directors, directors of nursing services, nurses trained to provide skilled nursing care, social workers, and activities directors. They are also required to hire as staff or retain as consultants:

- A pharmacist
- Therapists in a variety of specialties, including physical, occupational, and speech therapy
- Food service personnel, including a dietary supervisor
- An interdisciplinary assessment and assurance committee

Nursing facilities must be licensed under state law as nursing facilities. Assisted living facilities are not nursing homes. More than 80 percent of nursing homes also choose to participate in Medicare and Medicaid, which require nursing homes to meet strict federal certification standards on quality of care, quality of life, and residents' rights. For the purposes of this book and in general consumer usage, all licensed nursing facilities are considered skilled-care facilities. However, the federal government refers to non-Medicare-certified facilities as "nursing facilities" and to Medicare-certified facilities as "skilled nursing facilities," or "SNFs."

Either an entire facility or a portion of a facility can be licensed as a nursing facility. Continuing care retirement communities (CCRCs) and life care communities (LCCs) offer skilled nursing facility services for their residents. Some hospitals may also provide skilled nursing care in a long-term care unit.

Nursing facilities use personnel at a variety of training levels, which allows patient-care needs to be matched to appropriate training levels. Licensed nursing care levels include licensed practical nurse (LPN), registered nurse (RN), clinical nurse specialist (CNS), and registered nurse practitioner (RNP).

In addition to these types of licensed and registered nurses, almost all nursing facilities make heavy use of CNAs (certified nurse assistants or certified nurse aides) to provide most of the day-to-day basic services provided in a nursing home. CNAs may provide assistance with activities of daily living (ADLs) such as bathing, dressing, eating, toileting, transferring, and bowel/bladder incontinence, as well as assistance with instrumental ADLs (IADLs), which include housekeeping duties such as laundry and meal preparation. In general, CNAs must have a high school diploma or GED and must have completed a six- to twelve-week CNA certification program at a community college or medical facility. Classroom instruction in a certified nursing assistant program generally includes basic nursing skills, anatomy and physiology, nutrition, and infection control. Regulations on nursing assistant certification vary from state to state.

NURSING HOME GOALS

Nursing homes must provide services and activities to attain or maintain the highest practicable physical, mental, and psycho-social well-being of each resident in accordance with a written plan of care.

The goals of all nursing facilities are to (1) rehabilitate the resident to maximum potential and enable the resident to return to independent living arrangements if possible; (2) maintain maximum rehabilitation as long as possible within the realities of age and disease; (3) delay deterioration in physical and emotional well-being; and (4) support the resident and family, physically and emotionally, when health declines to the point of death. Nursing homes that receive federal funds must comply with federal legislation that calls for a high quality of care. Though all states must comply, at a minimum, with the federal regulations, some states have adopted tougher laws.

Congress enacted legislation in 1987 requiring nursing homes participating in the Medicare and Medicaid programs to comply with certain requirements for quality of care. This federal law, known as the Nursing Home Reform Act, specifies that a nursing home "must provide services and activities to attain or maintain the highest practicable physical, mental, and psychosocial well-being of each resident in accordance with a written plan of care . . ."

To participate in the Medicare and Medicaid programs, nursing homes must meet the following requirements:

- Have sufficient nursing staff. (42 CFR §483.30)
- Conduct initially a comprehensive and accurate assessment of each resident's functional capacity. (42 CFR §483.20)
- Develop a comprehensive care plan for each resident. (42 CFR §483.20)
- Prevent the deterioration of a resident's ability to bathe, dress, groom, transfer and ambulate, toilet, eat, and communicate. (42 CFR §483.25)
- Provide, if a resident is unable to carry out activities of daily living, the necessary services to maintain good nutrition, grooming, and personal oral hygiene. (42 CFR §483.25)
- Ensure that residents receive proper treatment and assistive devices to maintain vision and hearing abilities. (42 CFR §483.25)
- Ensure that residents do not develop pressure sores and, if a resident has pressure sores, provide the necessary treatment and services to promote healing, prevent infection, and prevent new sores from developing. (42 CFR §483.25)
- Provide appropriate treatment and services to incontinent residents to restore as much normal bladder functioning as possible. (42 CFR §483.25)
- Ensure that the resident receives adequate supervision and assistive devices to prevent accidents. (42 CFR §483.25)

- Maintain acceptable parameters of nutritional status. (42 CFR §483.25)
- Provide each resident with sufficient fluid intake to maintain proper hydration and health. (42 CFR §483.25)
- Ensure that residents are free of any significant medication errors. (42 CFR §483.25)
- Promote each resident's quality of life. (42 CFR §483.15)
- Maintain dignity and respect of each resident. (42 CFR §483.15)
- Ensure that the resident has the right to choose activities, schedules, and health care. (42 CFR §483.40)
- Provide pharmaceutical services to meet the needs of each resident. (42 CFR §483.60)
- Be administered in a manner that enables it [the nursing home] to use its resources effectively and efficiently. (42 CFR §483.75)
- Maintain accurate, complete, and easily accessible clinical records on each resident. (42 CFR §483.75)

CHAPTER 9

WHAT IS LONG-TERM CARE?

According to the American health-care system, long-term care differs from health care in that the goal of long-term care is not to cure an illness, but to allow an individual to attain and maintain an optimal level of functioning. Long-term care encompasses a wide array of medical, social, personal, and supportive and specialized housing services needed by individuals who have lost some capacity for self-care because of a chronic illness or disabling condition.

Long-term care encompasses a broad continuum of care:

- Medical care or skilled nursing care
- "Intermediate care" or "custodial care"—the type of care where people receive assistance with "activities of daily living" (toileting, bathing, dressing, eating, walking, transferring) or "instrumental activities of daily living" (things such as shopping, cooking, household chores, care of pets, and financial management)

- Supervision due to Alzheimer's disease or other forms of dementia

WHERE IS LONG-TERM CARE PROVIDED?

At Home
Home health care is provided in an individual's home (by family members or paid staff) and aims to keep the individual functioning at the highest possible level. Services range from basic assistance with household chores to skilled nursing services.

Assisted Living Facilities
An assisted living facility (ALF) typically provides apartment-style accommodations where services focus on providing assistance with ADLs and IADLs, including meals, housekeeping, medication assistance, laundry, and regular check-ins. ALFs are designed to bridge the gap between independent living and nursing home care.

Nursing Homes
As already explained, a nursing home is a medical facility that provides twenty-four-hour nursing care for people with serious illnesses or disabilities. The vast majority of all nursing homes are for-profit entities, and many of these are large corporations with nursing facilities in multiple states. Nursing homes generally provide three levels of service: rehabilitation for people who are injured, sick, or disabled; skilled nursing and medical care; and custodial care (help with eating, dressing, bathing, toileting, and moving about).

Adult Day Care
Adult day care programs provide meals and care services in a community setting during the day when a caregiver needs time off or must work.

Continuing Care Retirement Communities or Life Care Communities

Continuing care retirement communities (CCRCs) or life care communities (LCCs) provide a continuum of care from independent living through skilled nursing. The facilities allow individuals to live within the same community as their needs progress through the spectrum of care.

CHAPTER 10

DISCRIMINATION AGAINST CHRONIC ILLNESS

A chronic illness is a disease that is long-lasting or recurrent and needs to be managed on a long-term basis. According to various reports published by the Robert Wood Johnson Foundation, almost half of all Americans (roughly 150 million people) live with chronic illness, and people with chronic illness account for 83 percent of health-care spending.

According to the National Center for Chronic Disease Prevention and Health Promotion, part of the Centers for Disease Control and Prevention, chronic diseases—such as heart disease, diabetes, and arthritis—are among the most common, costly, and preventable of all health problems in the United States, and chronic illnesses such as these cause approximately 70 percent of deaths in the United States.

According to a 2004 report by the Bloomberg School of Public Health at the Johns Hopkins University (analyzing data from 1998), 85 percent of seniors (over age sixty-five) have at least one chronic disease, and 62 percent of them have two or more chronic illnesses. According to that same report, of adults between the ages of eighteen and sixty-four, 45 percent have at least one chronic disease, and 20 percent have two or more chronic illnesses.

WHY IS CHRONIC ILLNESS IMPORTANT?

The expenses of long-term care caused by a chronic illness are often catastrophic because Americans do not have a right to receive basic long-term care and therefore wind up paying privately for most long-term care. Through Medicare, seniors have had virtually universal health insurance coverage for *most* chronic illnesses since 1965. For individuals under age sixty-five, private health insurance has likewise always covered treatment, medication, and surgery for *most* chronic illnesses—such as heart disease, lung disease, kidney disease, and hundreds of other chronic medical conditions.

AMERICA'S HEALTH INSURANCE SYSTEM EFFECTIVELY DISCRIMINATES AGAINST CERTAIN CHRONIC ILLNESSES

The double tragedy of chronic illness is that our American health insurance system discriminates against people suffering from certain types of chronic illnesses, i.e., those that routinely result in the need for long-term care, such as Alzheimer's disease and other types of dementias; Parkinson's disease and other types of degenerative disorders of the central nervous system; Huntington's disease, amyotrophic lateral sclerosis (ALS), and other progressive neurodegenerative disorders; and many genetic disorders such as multiple sclerosis and muscular dystrophy. Those Americans suffering the tragedy of one of these diseases must also suffer the tragedy of having the "wrong" disease according to our American health insurance system. Is it an ethical social policy that seemingly arbitrarily distinguishes among these different types of illnesses? Is it an ethical social policy that provides full coverage for most illnesses—whether chronic or acute—but forces Americans with certain chronic conditions (many of them elders) to become impoverished in order to gain access to the long-term care necessitated by their particular type of chronic illness? Is it a surprise that Americans suffering the "wrong type" of chronic illness will want to look for legal ways to preserve the efforts of their lifetime in order to protect themselves from this unfair and seemingly arbitrary social policy?

CHAPTER 11

THE CAREGIVER'S ROLE

If you're reading this book, chances are good that you are either a caregiver or are facing the possibility of becoming a caregiver. Maybe you've been caring for your disabled spouse, or perhaps your aging parent is beginning to show signs of dementia. You're probably struggling with all kinds of difficult questions. Chances are that the person you're caring for never made any real plans for what to do in the event of physical disability or dementia.

Most family members who help their older loved ones don't see themselves as caregivers. Yet a caregiver is anyone who helps an older person with household chores, errands, personal care, or finances. Most caregivers also don't realize that caring for themselves is an important part of providing care for someone else. The simple truth is that you can't be a good caregiver if you don't take care of yourself.

If you have been taking care of your spouse, perhaps you are afraid of giving up the caregiver role, even if your own health may be deteriorating as a result of the stress of having to care for your spouse. If you are an adult child, perhaps you are worried about having to provide care for a parent with diminishing health and declining capacity. It is often very difficult for an adult child to step into a relationship reversal by taking over the parental role, but that is often exactly what happens—the child must become the parent, and the parent assumes the role of the child. This transition is fraught with conflict, confusion, and pain. If you're an adult child, most likely you have a career, children, and your own family and personal limitations to deal with. How can you possibly be expected to have to take care of your parents also?

Many conflicting thoughts and emotions arise when someone is confronted with having to care for an aging parent or a disabled spouse:

- **Love and Responsibility**: a desire to provide the best care for your spouse or for your parents.
- **Fear**: fear of losing your spouse or parent, fear of losing control, fear of the unknown, fear of not being able to conserve financial assets for future needs.
- **Confusion**: not knowing what long-term care options are available, how to get the best care, how much money will need to be spent on nursing care.
- **Guilt**: guilt for not being able to do more for your spouse or parent.
- **Anger and Frustration**: feelings of anger and frustration over the fact that your spouse or parent failed to plan ahead and foresee that this day might come.
- **Resentment**: resentment over why you are the one stuck being the primary caregiver.
- **Conflict**: constant arguments with a spouse or parent who has progressive dementia.
- **Self-preservation**: worry about how much of your own limited resources must be used to provide care for your spouse or parent.

All of these feelings are normal and are neither good nor bad. Give yourself a break; being a caregiver is hard, often underappreciated, work. Negative feelings do not mean you love the person any less. Allow yourself to feel how you feel and forgive yourself for any negative feelings.

CAREGIVER STRESS TEST

Which of the following are seldom true, sometimes true, often true, or usually true?

- I find I can't get enough rest.
- I don't have enough time for myself.
- I don't have enough time to be with family members other than the one I care for.
- I feel guilty about my situation.
- I don't get out much anymore.
- I have conflict with the person I take care of.
- I have conflicts with other family members.
- I cry a lot.
- I worry about having enough money to make ends meet.
- I don't feel I have enough knowledge or experience to give care as well as I'd like.
- I worry about my own health.

If the response to one or more of these areas is usually true or often true, it may be time to look for help with giving care and help with taking care of yourself.

CAREGIVER BURNOUT

According to WebMD,[1] Caregiver Burnout is a state of physical, emotional, and mental exhaustion that may be accompanied by a change in attitude—from positive and caring to negative and unconcerned. Burnout can occur when caregivers don't get the help they need, or if they try to do more than they are able to—either physically or financially. Caregivers who are "burned out" may experience fatigue, stress, anxiety, and depression.

---

[1] http://women.webmd.com/caregiver-recognizing-burnout

Caregivers often are so busy caring for others that they tend to neglect their own emotional, physical, and spiritual health. The demands on a caregiver's body, mind, and emotions can easily seem overwhelming, leading to fatigue and hopelessness—and, ultimately, burnout. Other factors that can lead to caregiver burnout include the following:

- Role confusion: you may be confused when thrust into the role of caregiver. It may be difficult for you to separate your role as caregiver from your role as spouse, lover, child, friend, etc.
- Unrealistic expectations: you may expect your involvement to have a positive effect on the health and happiness of the patient. This may be unrealistic for patients suffering from a progressive disease, such as Parkinson's or Alzheimer's.
- Lack of control: you may become frustrated by a lack of money, resources, and skills to effectively plan, manage, and organize your loved one's care.
- Unreasonable demands: you may place unreasonable burdens on yourself, in part because you see providing care as your exclusive responsibility.
- Other factors: you may not recognize when you are suffering burnout and eventually get to the point where you cannot function effectively. You may even become sick yourself.

SYMPTOMS OF CAREGIVER BURNOUT

According to WebMD,[2] the symptoms of caregiver burnout are similar to the symptoms of stress and depression:

- Withdrawal from friends, family, and other loved ones
- Loss of interest in activities previously enjoyed

---

[2] http://women.webmd.com/caregiver-recognizing-burnout

- Feeling blue, irritable, hopeless, and helpless
- Changes in appetite, weight, or both
- Changes in sleep patterns
- Getting sick more often
- Feelings of wanting to hurt yourself or the person for whom you are caring
- Emotional and physical exhaustion
- Irritability

WHAT YOU CAN DO TO TAKE CHARGE OF YOUR LIFE

Don't let your loved one's illness or disability always take center stage. While you might fall into a caregiving role because of an unexpected event, somewhere along the line you need to step back and consciously say, "I choose to take on this caregiving role." It goes a long way toward eliminating the feeling of being a victim.

Set realistic goals. Caregiving creates many conflicting demands on your time; it is vital to set realistic goals. Recognize what you can and cannot do. Define your priorities and stick to them as much as you can. You have the right to set limits and, though it is hard, it is okay to say no.

Seek out help from family and friends. When others offer assistance, accept it and suggest specific things they can do. Some caregivers see asking for help as a sign of weakness, failure, or inadequacy, when in fact it is just the opposite. Reaching out for assistance before you are beyond your limits is one characteristic of a strong person. While they might not be comfortable helping with bathing and dressing needs, friends and family can help by running errands, shopping for groceries, preparing meals, or just visiting. They can call regularly, taking some pressure off you to be the primary social outlet.

Seek out appropriate geriatric medical professionals. A geriatrician is a medical doctor who is specially trained to prevent and manage the unique health concerns of older adults.

Older persons may react to illness and disease differently from younger adults. Geriatricians are able to treat older patients, manage multiple disease symptoms, and develop care plans that address the special health-care needs of older adults. Geriatricians are typically primary care physicians who are board-certified in either family practice or internal medicine and have also acquired the additional training necessary to obtain the Certificate of Added Qualifications in Geriatric Medicine. You can locate a geriatrician in your area through the website of either the American Medical Association (www.ama-assn.org) or the American Board of Family Medicine (www.theabfm.org).

Seek out the assistance of an Aging Life Care Manager. Aging life care professionals are professionals with degrees in one or more fields of human services (e.g., social work, psychology, nursing, or gerontology) who specialize in assisting older people and their families with long-term care arrangements. Aging life care professionals are typically independent from the resources they recommend, so they can provide an unbiased assessment of each situation. Aging life care professionals can work with families and elders prior to the need for services and can also assist in emergency situations. You can locate an aging life care professional in your area through the website of Aging Life Care Association at www.aginglifecare.org.

Investigate community and professional resources such as in-home health services or adult daycare. Employ a home health aide to cook, clean, and help with bathing, eating, dressing, using the bathroom, and getting around the house. Check your local phone book or search the Internet for "home health-care providers." These are the types of services that an older parent should expect to have to pay for if they are not available for free in the community.

When you just need a short break, consider respite care. You can hire a companion to stay with your care-receiver for a few hours at a time on a regular basis to give you some time off. In addition, most nursing homes and assisted living facilities offer families the opportunity to place older relatives in their facilities for short stays. Your local area's agency on aging can help with arrangements.

CHAPTER 12

SELECTING A FACILITY

Most nursing home admissions happen under a great deal of stress. There are generally two ways a nursing admission takes place: either directly from home to a nursing facility or via discharge from a hospital to a nursing facility for short-term rehabilitation.

In order to get admitted directly from home to a nursing facility, a family member typically must call the local nursing facilities to determine if they have openings. Calling the local nursing facilities every day, first thing in the morning, is often the best way to find an opening. Even if a nursing facility says they will add your loved one to a waiting list, persistence in calling every day is often rewarded because if an opening is available, it is easier for the nursing home admission staff to say "come on over" rather than face the prospect of calling down a waiting list and perhaps spending hours before finding someone who is ready to move in that day.

A rehabilitation (rehab) discharge occurs when an individual has been admitted to a hospital for an acute injury or illness, has remained hospitalized for at least three days, and is then transferred directly from the hospital to a nursing facility for short-term rehabilitation (physical therapy, speech therapy, etc.). Not only is this the easier way of getting into a nursing home, but it also has the advantage of being a type of short-term rehabilitation, which will be covered primarily by Medicare. See page 103 for more information about Medicare-covered rehabilitation.

A rehab discharge often occurs with the assistance of a hospital "case manager" (sometimes called a "discharge planner"), who is typically a nurse or a social worker. Case managers have general information about nursing facilities near the hospital, but they normally don't have time to learn about the actual quality of care in a given facility. In some jurisdictions, there is an area-wide computer system whereby hospital case managers can simply send out a request to area nursing facilities to see which facility has an opening for the patient needing rehab.

Regardless of whether you are admitting your loved one to a nursing facility directly from home or via a rehab discharge, you may be faced with the overwhelming task of finding the best nursing home for a loved one. It is easier, and better for your loved one, if the first placement is to the best possible facility. Although a nursing home resident can be moved from one facility to another, this type of disruption can be very disturbing and is rarely in everyone's best interest.

WHERE DO YOU BEGIN?

To get the best possible nursing home, the first step is for the family and/or potential resident to determine what is most important to them in looking for a facility. The resident's needs and desires must be included in this evaluation. Variables such as location of the facility, whether a special care unit is available, and what types of payment sources are accepted should also be considered when beginning this process.

The next step is to identify the facilities in your area that meet the criteria you have established. If placement is not urgent, you can contact each nursing facility in your nearby area and ask for its information packet, which should include an activity calendar and a menu. You should also ask for the three most recent state annual inspection reports detailing the facility's major and minor deficiencies; nursing homes are required to make these reports available upon request. Virtually every nursing home will have some deficiencies; after all, working with extremely disabled and impaired persons is very difficult. Your local Area Agency on Aging should also have resources and helpful aids for assisting you in finding and comparing nursing homes.

The most helpful of all resources is Medicare's Nursing Home Quality Compare website at www.medicare.gov/NHCompare. Here, you can obtain detailed inspection information about each nursing facility that interests you, comparing various government-rated "quality measures" such as percent of residents who have moderate to severe pain, percent of high-risk residents who have pressure sores, percent of residents who were physically restrained, and percent of residents who spend most of their time in bed or in a chair. The NHCompare website also rates the care and services that each facility provides to its residents and allows you to view how each facility stacks up in staffing hours for each type of health-care worker against state and national averages. The NHCompare website also tells you whether each facility accepts Medicare and Medicaid.

Step three is to tour the facilities you have identified in step two. Assuming you're interested in Medicaid asset protection, which will be discussed starting on page 105, then limit your search to those nursing homes that accept Medicaid, which is almost all nursing homes. There is no need to schedule your visits in advance (even though some nursing homes prefer this). Just show up during regular business hours. You should be able to meet with an administrative staff member, who should be able to answer all your questions. You will also want to tour a second time, in the evening or on the weekend, to see if there is a drastic difference in the atmosphere of the facility or the care being provided. It is important to tour at least two facilities so you can see the difference in the physical plant and the staff.

While you are touring the facility, pay attention to your gut feeling. Ask yourself how you feel about the environment:

- Do I feel welcome?
- How long did I have to wait to meet with someone?
- Did the admissions director ask about my family member's wants and needs?
- Is the facility clean?
- Are there any strong odors?
- Are the staff friendly?
- Do they seem to genuinely care for the residents?
- Do the staff seem to get along with one another?

Listen and Observe

You can learn a lot just by watching and paying attention—and asking questions. You want to be sure that the facility is giving proactive care, not just reacting to crisis. Here are a few examples of the types of questions the staff should be able to answer:

- How do you ensure that call lights are answered promptly, regardless of your staffing?
- If my father is not able to move or turn himself, how do you ensure that he is turned and does not develop bedsores?
- How do you make sure that someone is assisted with the activities of daily living such as dressing, toileting, and transferring?
- Can residents bring in their own supplies?
- Can residents use any pharmacy they wish?
- How many direct-care staff members do you have on each shift? Does this number exceed the minimal num-

ber that state regulations require, or do you just meet the minimum standard?

- What sources of payment do you accept?
- How long has the medical director been with your facility?
- How were your last state survey results? (Get a copy.)
- How did you correct any deficiencies and what process did you put in place to make sure you do not make these mistakes again?
- Has the state prohibited this facility from accepting new residents at any time during the last two years?
- What is your policy on family care-planning conferences? Will you adjust your schedule to make sure that I can attend the meeting?
- Do you have a list of references with whom I can talk?
- Can my loved one come in for a meal to see if he/she fits in and likes the facility?

Beginning on page 92, you will find a comprehensive Nursing Home Evaluation Tool you can use when touring facilities. This tool will help you keep track of which facility you like best. You should make a separate copy of the blank form for each facility you plan to visit.

CHAPTER 13

NURSING HOME EVALUATION TOOL

As you visit nursing homes, use the following form for each place you visit. Don't expect every nursing home to score well on every question. The presence or absence of any of these items does not automatically mean a facility is good or bad. Each has its own strengths and weaknesses. Simply consider what is most important to the resident and you.

Record your observations for each question by circling a number from one to five. If a question is unimportant to you or doesn't apply to your loved one, leave the evaluation area for that question blank. Then total all numbers circled for each facility.

Your ratings will help you compare nursing homes and choose the best one for your situation. The facilities with the highest scores are those on which you should ultimately focus your attention. However, you shouldn't rely solely on the numbers. Ask to speak to family members of other residents. Also, contact the local or state ombudsman for information about the nursing home and get a copy of the facility's state inspection report from the nursing home, the agency that licenses nursing homes, or the ombudsman.

Nursing Home Evaluation Tool

Name of Nursing Home: _____

Date Visited: _____

Rating Scale				
Un-acceptable	Acceptable	Average	Above Average	Excellent
1	2	3	4	5

THE BUILDING AND ITS SURROUNDINGS:

What is your first impression of the facility?	1 2 3 4 5
What is the condition of the facility's exterior paint, gutters, and trim?	1 2 3 4 5
Are the grounds pleasant and well kept?	1 2 3 4 5
Do you like the view from residents' rooms and other windows?	1 2 3 4 5
Are there appropriate areas for physical therapy and occupational therapy?	1 2 3 4 5
Do chairs and other furniture seem sturdy and difficult to tip? Are they attractive and comfortable?	1 2 3 4 5
Do patient beds in double rooms have privacy curtains?	1 2 3 4 5
Are there curtains being used by staff to protect the privacy of patients receiving treatments or assistance?	1 2 3 4 5
Is an on-site barber or beauty salon available?	1 2 3 4 5
Is an on-site library available?	1 2 3 4 5

Is an on-site computer center with high speed Internet access available?	1 2 3 4 5
Is an on-site gift shop available?	1 2 3 4 5
Is an on-site general store available?	1 2 3 4 5
Do meals appear appetizing and are they served promptly at the proper times?	1 2 3 4 5
Do residents who need help eating receive adequate assistance?	1 2 3 4 5
Is the dining area clean and pleasant?	1 2 3 4 5
Is there room at and between tables for both residents and aides for those who need assistance with meals?	1 2 3 4 5
What is the level and enthusiasm of resident participation in the activities?	1 2 3 4 5
Is there a well-ventilated indoor room for smokers?	1 2 3 4 5
Is there a covered/enclosed outdoor shelter for smokers?	1 2 3 4 5
Are nonsmoking rules enforced, both indoors and outdoors, in all nonsmoking areas?	1 2 3 4 5
What is your impression of general cleanliness throughout the facility?	1 2 3 4 5
What is your impression of the general cleanliness and grooming of residents?	1 2 3 4 5
Does the facility smell clean?	1 2 3 4 5
Is there enough space in resident rooms and common areas for the number of residents?	1 2 3 4 5
How noisy are hallways and common areas?	1 2 3 4 5
Are common areas such as lounges and activity rooms provided?	1 2 3 4 5
Are residents allowed to bring furniture and other personal items to decorate their rooms?	1 2 3 4 5

Do residents with Alzheimer's disease live in a separate Alzheimer's unit?	1 2 3 4 5
Does the facility provide a secure outdoor area?	1 2 3 4 5
Is there a secure area where a resident with Alzheimer's can safely wander on paths?	1 2 3 4 5

THE STAFF, POLICIES, AND PRACTICES:

Does the administrator know residents by name and speak to them in a pleasant, friendly way?	1 2 3 4 5
Do staff and residents communicate with cheerful, respectful attitudes?	1 2 3 4 5
Do staff and administration seem to work well with one another in a spirit of cooperation?	1 2 3 4 5
Do residents get permanent assignment of staff?	1 2 3 4 5
Do nursing assistants participate in the residents' care planning process?	1 2 3 4 5
How good is the facility's record for employee retention?	1 2 3 4 5
Does a state ombudsman visit the facility on a regular basis?	1 2 3 4 5
How likely is an increase in private-pay rates?	1 2 3 4 5
Are there any additional charges not included in the daily or monthly rate?	1 2 3 4 5

QUESTIONS TO ASK THE STAFF:

Are beds available?	1 2 3 4 5
What method is used in matching roommates?	1 2 3 4 5
What is a typical day like?	1 2 3 4 5
Can residents choose what time to go to bed and wake up?	1 2 3 4 5

Are meaningful activities available that are appropriate for residents?	1 2 3 4 5
Is there an activities schedule posted? Are residents engaged in activities?	1 2 3 4 5
Can residents continue to participate in interests such as gardening or contact with pets?	1 2 3 4 5
Does the facility provide transportation for religious services and other activities?	1 2 3 4 5
Is a van or bus with wheelchair access available?	1 2 3 4 5
How are decisions about method and frequency of bathing made?	1 2 3 4 5
How do residents get their clothes laundered?	1 2 3 4 5
What happens when clothing or other items are missing?	1 2 3 4 5
Does the facility have a current license from the state?	1 2 3 4 5
Does the administrator have a current license from the state?	1 2 3 4 5
If Medicare and/or Medicaid coverage is needed, is the facility certified?	1 2 3 4 5
Does the facility have a formal quality assurance program?	1 2 3 4 5
Does the facility have an operating agreement with a nearby hospital for emergencies?	1 2 3 4 5
Is a physician available in an emergency?	1 2 3 4 5
Are personal physicians allowed?	1 2 3 4 5
How is regular medical attention assured?	1 2 3 4 5
How are patients and families involved in treatment plans?	1 2 3 4 5
Are specialty medical services available (e.g., dentists, podiatrists, optometrists)?	1 2 3 4 5
Does the facility report to the patient's personal physician on progress? To families?	1 2 3 4 5

What services are provided for terminally ill patients and their families?	1 2 3 4 5
Is a licensed nurse always available?	1 2 3 4 5
Does a pharmacist review patient drug regimens?	1 2 3 4 5
Are arrangements made for patients to worship or attend religious services?	1 2 3 4 5
Is physical therapy available under the direction of a licensed physical therapist?	1 2 3 4 5
Are services of an occupational therapist or speech pathologist available?	1 2 3 4 5
How are residents encouraged to participate in activities?	1 2 3 4 5
How are patient activity preferences respected?	1 2 3 4 5
Are both group and individual activities available?	1 2 3 4 5
Is a social worker available to assist residents and families?	1 2 3 4 5
Does a dietician plan menus for patients on special diets?	1 2 3 4 5
Are personal likes and dislikes taken into consideration in menu planning?	1 2 3 4 5
Are snacks available between meals?	1 2 3 4 5
Are the number of meals/snacks provided adequate?	1 2 3 4 5
Is the food preparation area separate from the dishwashing and garbage areas?	1 2 3 4 5
Is food that needs refrigeration put away promptly, and not left standing on counters?	1 2 3 4 5
Is there fresh water on bedside stands?	1 2 3 4 5
Are there handrails in hallways and grab bars in bathrooms?	1 2 3 4 5
Are toilets convenient to bedrooms?	1 2 3 4 5
Is there a sink in each bathroom?	1 2 3 4 5
Are call bells near each toilet?	1 2 3 4 5

Are the hallways wide enough to accommodate passing wheelchairs?	1 2 3 4 5
Are the rooms large enough to allow a wheelchair to maneuver easily?	1 2 3 4 5
Is the temperature comfortable (remember, many seniors prefer warmer environments)?	1 2 3 4 5
Does every patient room have a window?	1 2 3 4 5
Do all residents have closets and drawers for clothing?	1 2 3 4 5
Is the atmosphere generally friendly and welcoming?	1 2 3 4 5
If residents call out for help or use a call light, do they get prompt, appropriate responses?	1 2 3 4 5
Does each resident have the same nursing assistant(s) most of the time?	1 2 3 4 5
How does a resident with problems voice a complaint?	1 2 3 4 5
How are disputes, problems, or complaints with the quality of care resolved?	1 2 3 4 5
Are residents who are able to permitted to participate in care-plan meetings?	1 2 3 4 5
Does the facility have an effective resident council?	1 2 3 4 5
Is an effective family council in place?	1 2 3 4 5
Can family/staff meetings be scheduled to discuss and work out any problems that may arise?	1 2 3 4 5

QUESTIONS TO ASK YOURSELF:

Do I feel comfortable coming here/leaving my loved one here?	1 2 3 4 5
How convenient is the facility's location to me and other family members who may want to visit the resident?	1 2 3 4 5

Are there areas other than the resident's room where family members can visit?	1 2 3 4 5
Does the facility have safe, well-lighted, convenient parking?	1 2 3 4 5
Are hotels/motels nearby for out-of-town family members?	1 2 3 4 5
Are there restaurants nearby suitable for taking the resident out for meals with family members?	1 2 3 4 5
How convenient will care-planning conferences be for interested family members?	1 2 3 4 5
Is the facility convenient for the patient's personal physician?	1 2 3 4 5

Total Score: _____

CHAPTER 14

HOW TO PAY FOR NURSING HOME CARE

One of the greatest concerns people have about nursing home care is how to pay for it. There are basically four ways to pay for the cost of the care provided by a nursing home.

PRIVATE PAY

This is the method many people must use at first. It means paying for the cost of a nursing home out of your own pocket. Unfortunately, with nursing home bills of more than $12,000 per month at some facilities, few people can afford to pay on their own for a long-term stay in a nursing home. Even those who can afford to do so often desire to explore other options— options that allow them to retain some or all of their assets for other important needs, while still permitting them to pay for nursing home care.

LONG-TERM CARE INSURANCE

If you have long-term care insurance coverage, this could help pay the costs of needed home care or nursing home care. Unfortunately, only about 10 percent of the population carry long-term care insurance, so most people facing a nursing home stay do not have this type of coverage in place. Many people who would like to purchase this type of coverage find that they cannot afford it. How to purchase the best long-term care policy is a complicated subject that is well worth exploring if you are in your fifties or sixties and still healthy. It should be given serious consideration if it is affordable for you, especially in view of the new federally mandated "Long-Term Care Partnership," which allows you to use long-term care insurance as a type of Medicaid asset protection—allowing you to protect assets equivalent to the premium paid for the insurance. If you are thinking about purchasing a long-term care insurance policy, an experienced elder law attorney can assist you in finding the best policy by helping you compare and contrast the numerous types of policies available and the different types and levels of coverage offered, as well as the independent ratings and financial stability of the insurance company providing the coverage. You should also discuss some of the uses of, and alternatives to, long-term care insurance with an elder law attorney, so that you have a better understanding of the cost versus benefit of such coverage and of the multitude of options to pay for long-term care besides traditional long-term care insurance. Try to find an elder law attorney who is also licensed to sell long-term care insurance and other types of insurance and annuity products that can help cover the expenses of long-term care. You will find additional information in Chapter 17: Long-Term Care Insurance starting on page 109.

DEPARTMENT OF VETERANS AFFAIRS

The Department of Veterans Affairs (VA) primarily pays for long-term care through the Veterans "Aid and Attendance" Special Pension Benefit payments. In some parts of the country, there are also nursing homes that are run by the Department of Veterans Affairs. You will find additional information about the

Veterans "Aid and Attendance" Special Pension in the chapter on that topic starting on page 117.

MEDICAID

This is a combined federally funded and state-funded benefit program, administered by each state, that can pay for the cost of a nursing home if certain asset and income tests are met. According to AARP, about 70 percent of nursing home residents are supported, at least in part, by Medicaid. Medicaid qualification and eligibility will be discussed in greater detail starting on page 123.

A WORD ABOUT MEDICARE

You will notice that Medicare is *not* listed among the sources of funds used to pay for long-term care in a nursing home. This is because Medicare does not pay a penny for long-term care, ever. Medicare is the national health insurance program primarily for people sixty-five years of age and older, those under age sixty-five who have been disabled for at least twenty-four months, and people with kidney failure. Medicare may provide some coverage for short-term (up to one hundred days) rehabilitation in a nursing facility, provided you continue to get better from the rehabilitation, but you must meet certain strict qualification rules, which will be discussed in greater detail in the next chapter.

CHAPTER 15

WHAT DOES MEDICARE COVER?

Most people have a great deal of confusion between Medicare and Medicaid.

Medicare is a federally funded and federally administered health insurance program, primarily designed for individuals over age sixty-five. Medicare does not cover long-term care under any circumstances.

If you are enrolled in a traditional Medicare plan, and you've been in the hospital at least three days, and you are admitted directly from the hospital into a rehab facility (which are typically skilled nursing facilities) for short-term rehabilitation (i.e., therapy and treatment designed to make you better), then Medicare should pay the full cost of this short-term rehab stay for the first twenty days and may continue to pay part of the cost of the short-term rehab stay for the next eighty days—with a per day deductible that you must pay privately (although there are Medicare supplement insurance policies that sometimes cover that deductible). There is also a Medicare Managed Care plan, for which the three-day hospital stay may not be required, and for which the deductible for days twenty-one through one hundred is waived, provided certain strict qualifying rules are met. But whether the plan is traditional Medicare or Medicare Managed Care (MMC), the nursing home resident must be receiving daily rehabilitative care and must be improving. Medicare does not pay for long-term care (i.e., for custodial nursing home stays or in-home care).

In a best-case scenario, traditional Medicare or MMC will provide some coverage for the hospital stay and rehabilitation of up to one hundred days for each "spell of illness" (although in our experience coverage usually falls far short of the one-hundred-day maximum). If you recover sufficiently that you do not require a Medicare-covered care benefit for sixty consecutive days, you may be eligible for another benefit period (i.e., another one hundred days of Medicare coverage), but the illness or disorder must *not* be a chronic degenerative condition from which you will not recover.

What happens if you've used up the one hundred days of coverage and still need more rehabilitation, or if you need to move into long-term nursing home care? You're back to one of the alternatives outlined previously: long-term care insurance, paying the bills with your own assets, VA assistance, or qualifying for Medicaid.

CHAPTER 16

WHY MEDICAID PLANNING IS ETHICAL

Medicaid asset protection is absolutely ethical and moral; in fact, it is the "right" thing to do if a family is concerned about the long-term care of a loved one. From a moral and ethical standpoint, Medicaid planning is no different from income tax planning and estate planning.

MEDICAID PLANNING IS JUST LIKE INCOME TAX PLANNING

Income tax planning involves trying to find all of the proper and legal deductions, credits, and other tax savings that you are entitled to—taking maximum advantage of existing laws. Income tax planning also involves investing in tax-free bonds, retirement plans, or other tax-favored investment vehicles, all in an effort to minimize what you pay in income taxes and maximize the amount of money that remains in your control to be used to benefit you and your family.

MEDICAID PLANNING IS JUST LIKE ESTATE PLANNING

Estate planning involves trying to plan your estate to minimize the amount of estate taxes and probate taxes that your estate will have to pay to the government, again taking maximum advantage of the existing laws. Similarly, Medicaid planning involves trying to find the best methods to transfer, shelter, and protect your assets to get the same benefits of lowering costs and keeping control of your money and benefits.

Like income-tax planning and estate planning, Medicaid planning requires a great deal of extremely complex knowledge due in part to constantly changing laws, so you need to work with an experienced elder law attorney who knows the rules and can advise you properly.

MEDICAID PLANNING IS JUST LIKE LONG-TERM CARE INSURANCE

For seniors over the age of sixty-five, Medicaid has become equivalent to federally subsidized long-term care insurance, just as Medicare is equivalent to federally subsidized health insurance. Congress accepts the realities of Medicaid planning through rules that protect spouses of nursing home residents, allow Medicaid asset protection via the purchase of qualified long-term care insurance policies, allow the exemption of certain types of assets, and permit individuals to qualify even after transferring assets to a spouse or to a disabled family member or to a caregiver child. To plan ahead and accelerate qualification for Medicaid is no different from planning to maximize your income tax deductions to receive the largest income tax refund allowable. It's no different from taking advantage of tax-free municipal bonds. It's no different from planning your estate to avoid paying estate taxes.

MEDICAID PLANNING IS JUST LIKE MAGIC

The "magic" that elder law attorneys are able to perform is not based on sleight of hand. Elder law attorneys do not "hide" assets. On the contrary, we provide total disclosure of everything we do to the relevant Medicaid agencies when we file the Medicaid application, as failure to provide full disclosure of all assets and all transfers would be a federal crime. The ways that elder law attorneys are able to shelter and protect assets may seem like "magic" to you, but that's only because you don't possess the legal knowledge and experience. It's the same with magicians—the magic only appears to be "magical" because you don't know how the trick is done. Just as magicians study and train for years to become good at their craft, elder law attorneys also study and train for years to become experts in their field. To become a certified elder law attorney, attorneys must: spend an average of at least sixteen hours per week practicing elder law during the three years preceding their application; must handle a minimum of sixty elder law matters, in thirteen different areas of elder law, during those three years; participate in at least forty-five hours of continuing legal education in elder law during the preceding three years; submit five references from attorneys familiar with their competence and qualifications in elder law; and must pass a full-day certification examination (one of the most recent exams had a 19 percent pass rate). Done with respect for the law and compassion for the elders that are being protected, Medicaid planning is not only ethically justified, it is often imperative to the individual's quality of life.

MEDICAID ASSET PROTECTION IS NEEDED BECAUSE OUR HEALTH-CARE SYSTEM IS DISCRIMINATORY

Within the United States, no one yet has a right to basic long-term care. We give seniors virtually universal coverage only for certain types of health problems. Treatment and surgery for health conditions such as heart disease, lung disease, kidney disease, bone disease, cancer, and hundreds of other medical conditions will not impoverish most seniors because Medicare and private health insurance cover these diseases, and we all pay our fair share for such coverage. But neither Medicare nor private health insurance covers chronic illnesses such as Alzheimer's disease or other types of brain diseases causing dementia or loss of the ability to function independently. For these types of diseases, seniors must become officially "impoverished" under federal and state Medicaid rules in order to gain access to basic long-term care. Is this an ethical social policy that arbitrarily distinguishes among these different types of diseases? Is this an ethical social policy that provides full coverage for most diseases but forces elders with certain conditions to become impoverished in order to gain access to basic long-term care? Is it a surprise to anyone that most seniors will want to look for legal ways to preserve the efforts of their lifetime in order to protect themselves from this unfair and arbitrary social policy? Medicaid planning is not about "cheating" or "gaming" the system; it is about preserving a client's dignity and self-worth in the face of an unfair and arbitrary social policy. The ethical scandal is America's public policy, not the desire of seniors to avoid poverty.

CHAPTER 17

LONG-TERM CARE INSURANCE

Long-term care insurance, for some people, can be a good way to provide for future long-term care needs. If you have long-term care insurance coverage, this could help pay the costs of nursing home care. Unfortunately, only about 10 percent of the population carry long-term care insurance, so most people facing a nursing home stay do not have this type of coverage in place. Many people who would like to purchase this type of coverage find that they cannot afford it.

However, this type of insurance coverage is worth exploring if you are under the age of sixty-five and still healthy, especially in view of the federally mandated "Long-Term Care Partnership," which allows you to use special long-term care insurance for Medicaid asset protection to protect an amount of assets equivalent to the total amount of insurance coverage you purchase.

If you are thinking about purchasing a long-term care insurance policy, an experienced, independent insurance agent who specializes in long-term care insurance can assist you in finding the best policy by helping you compare and contrast the numerous types of policies available and the different types and levels of coverage offered, as well as the independent ratings and financial stability of the insurance company providing the coverage. The two big downsides of traditional long-term care insurance is that (1) these policies are "use or lose," and (2) the fact that, historically, the premiums for these policies have drastically increased after someone purchases a policy. Accordingly, most people are better off considering hybrid products that combine a life insurance policy or an annuity with a long-term care benefit. There are even products that allow you to effectively use tax-free dollars to pay for long-term care coverage through a provision in the Pension Protection Act.

Additionally, you should discuss some of the alternatives to long-term care insurance with a qualified elder law attorney so that you have a better understanding of the cost versus benefit of such coverage. Elder law attorneys are uniquely qualified to assess and address *all* of the issues that a client needing long-term care will face. Very few insurance agents have a complete understanding of nursing home laws and Medicaid asset protection strategies, and are therefore not able to adequately address all of the issues and options surrounding how to pay for long-term care. On the other hand, many experienced elder law attorneys are also licensed to sell long-term care insurance and other products that help pay for long-term care, such as hybrid life insurance and hybrid annuity products that offer a long-term care benefit. This type of elder law attorney can explain and offer you both legal-based asset protection strategies and financial-based asset protection strategies and help you determine which strategies make the most sense for your specific situation.

WHAT ELDER LAW ISSUES MUST BE CONSIDERED WHEN PURCHASING LONG-TERM CARE INSURANCE?

When shopping for a long-term care insurance product, it is crucial to consider carefully the entire financial situation of both spouses and to consider the possible alternative of not purchasing long-term care insurance. Failure to do so can result in purchasing too little coverage, too much coverage, or coverage for the wrong spouse, each of which can actually be worse than purchasing no coverage at all.

Example of Purchasing Too Little Coverage

Consider Joe and Linda, a married couple facing Joe's nursing home costs of $8,500 per month. Joe has $4,000 in monthly retirement income, as well as a long-term care insurance policy with a monthly benefit of $4,500 (based on a daily benefit of $150). Linda's only income is social security, which is $700 per month. At first glance, the couple seems better off with the long-term care policy; they have an extra $4,500 per month, without which they could not afford the nursing home. With the insurance, Joe has exactly enough income to pay the private rate of the nursing home. Unfortunately, Linda's monthly expenses, even with Joe in the nursing home, are approximately $2,200 per month, and Joe is not eligible for Medicaid assistance because his income (including the long-term care insurance benefit) is sufficient to pay the private nursing home bill.

In this example, Joe's long-term care insurance policy does not provide enough of a benefit to allow Linda to have sufficient income to meet her needs. If Joe's long-term care insurance policy had provided a $6,000 monthly benefit ($200 per day instead of $150), then Joe would have income of $10,000 per month, and $1,500 of Joe's retirement income would be available for Linda's monthly expenses. Joe's extra $1,500 per month plus Linda's own $700 per month would be just enough income for Linda to live on. Joe and Linda could have fully financed Joe's long-term care needs and ensured that Linda would have enough funds to meet her monthly expenses.

If Joe and Linda had recognized this shortfall and decided to not purchase the long-term care insurance, or if they could not afford the increased premiums for the increased monthly benefit, they could instead use Medicaid assistance to help pay for Joe's nursing home costs. Most of Joe's $4,000 monthly income would normally be required to pay the nursing home expenses; Linda would keep her $700 per month. However, because Linda's income is so low, the Medicaid rules would allow Linda to receive part of Joe's income to help her with her monthly living expenses. Linda could receive a monthly maintenance needs allowance of up to $2,841[3] (including her income), which includes allowances for housing and utilities. Therefore, in this case, Joe and Linda would have the nursing home costs paid, and Linda would have up to $2,841 monthly for her support.

The bottom line? Either buy enough long-term care insurance coverage or don't buy any. It doesn't make sense to pay insurance premiums and then be bankrupted by nursing home fees anyway because of insufficient coverage. And if you do buy coverage, be sure to get adequate inflation coverage. As with other medical expenses, the inflation rate in nursing home fees is currently quite high. In ten years, the cost of the nursing homes, at the current rate of inflation, will be about twice what it is today.

Which Spouse Should Get Coverage?

Often a married couple will be able to afford coverage for only one spouse. *Statistics alone* would dictate that the wife should purchase the policy, as women tend to live longer than men and are therefore more likely than men to end up in a nursing home for a long period of time. However, this is often the wrong answer! For a couple whose husband's retirement income is much higher than the wife's, it is actually much more important to purchase coverage for the husband. As was the case with Joe and Linda, if the husband enters the nursing home without adequate long-term care coverage, the wife may wind up destitute or without sufficient income to live on.

---

[3] This is the maximum monthly maintenance needs allowance as of May, 2012.

The other half of the story is what happens if the wife goes into the nursing home first. Using the same fact scenario, let's now assume that Linda enters the nursing home first and does not have long-term care coverage. Is there any problem? No, not at all, because we can get Linda's nursing home paid for almost entirely through Medicaid assistance. Linda's $700 monthly income would have to go to the nursing home, but Medicaid will pay the rest. Joe will be able to keep 100 percent of his retirement income and, with proper Medicaid asset protection planning, will be able to keep all of his assets.

How Much Coverage Do I Need?

I don't recommend anyone purchasing more than five years of long-term care insurance coverage. One reason is that the average nursing home stay is only approximately three years. Second, after moving to a nursing home, your family can commence the process of Medicaid asset protection, which is the primary focus of my practice as an elder law attorney. Using Medicaid asset protection, we can have you transfer your assets into a special type of asset protection trust. After five years have passed, if you are still alive, you'll be able to qualify for Medicaid to pay your nursing home costs (provided the assets remaining in your name do not exceed Medicaid's limits). Using this strategy, you'll only need long-term care coverage for five years before Medicaid coverage commences, so there's no need to purchase more than five years of long-term care coverage.

How Do I Know If I Can Afford LTC Insurance?

You should generally only purchase long-term care insurance if you can pay the premiums out of your disposable income (i.e., if the premiums are affordable using income that you would otherwise add to your savings).

How Can I Reduce My Premium?

There are five ways to reduce the cost of LTC insurance. First, request a one-hundred-day elimination period, since Medicare may pay some or all of the first one hundred days (to the extent skilled nursing care is required). Second, the daily benefit purchased can be reduced by income from pensions and social security, to the extent these items may not be needed by a spouse. Third, the benefit period should be limited to five years, because this will encompass the majority of claims, and the Medicaid look-back period for transfers does not exceed that period. Fourth, work with an independent agent who can provide at least three premium quotes. Some clients end up paying too much due to transactions with captive agents. Fifth, the cost of the insurance may be reduced significantly by purchasing a hybrid product that combines a life insurance policy or an annuity with a long-term care benefit. As mentioned earlier, you can find products that allow you to use tax-free dollars to pay for long-term care coverage through a provision in the Pension Protection Act.

When Is the Best Time to Purchase Coverage?

If you decide that long-term care insurance is the right decision to protect your assets and your family's financial future, the best time to buy it is now, because the older you get, the more expensive the policy becomes in the long run. By buying now:

- You avoid the risk of needing care you will have to pay for yourself.
- You avoid the risk of developing a condition that would make you uninsurable later.
- You pay lower premiums now, rather than paying higher premiums later.

The following sample table shows the cost for a forty-four-year-old male if he waits and buys later, assuming that premiums do not change and the applicant remains insurable. The Daily Benefit is increased 5 percent for each year of waiting, to cover the increased cost of care over time.

Age at Purchase	Daily Benefit	Premium	Premiums Paid to Age 90	Cost of Waiting
44	$200	$1,598	$73,508	$0
46	$221	$1,893	$83,292	$9,784
48	$243	$2,232	$93,730	$20,222
50	$268	$2,643	$105,707	$32,199
52	$295	$3,039	$115,487	$41,979
54	$326	$3,489	$125,607	$52,099

What Benefits and Riders Are Most Important?

The most important benefits are inflation protection, as mentioned above, and a stay-at-home option. Some long-term care insurance policies limit the amount of home-care coverage. For example, a policy may pay $200 per day for nursing home care, but only $150 per day for home care; this is an example of a 75 percent home-care benefit. Given that almost everyone needing long-term care prefers to remain in his or her own home for as long as possible, a 100 percent home-care benefit is an essential option.

Tax Deductibility of Long-Term Care Insurance Premiums

Federal Income Tax: Under the Health Insurance Portability and Accountability Act (HIPAA), "qualified" long-term care insurance policies receive special tax treatment. To be "qualified," policies must adhere to regulations established by the National Association of Insurance Commissioners:

- The policy must offer the consumer the options of "inflation" and "nonforfeiture" protection, although the consumer can choose not to purchase these features.
- The policies must also offer both activities of daily living (ADL) and cognitive impairment triggers but may not

offer a medical necessity trigger. "Triggers" are conditions that must be present for a policy to be activated.

- Premiums for "qualified" long-term care policies will be treated as a medical expense and will be deductible from federal income tax to the extent that they, along with other unreimbursed medical expenses (including "Medigap" insurance premiums), exceed 10 percent of the insured's adjusted gross income. But the deductibility of premiums is limited by the age of the taxpayer at the end of the year.

State Income Tax: Many states have programs allowing a deduction from state income taxes.

Might the LTC Insurance Company Go out of Business?

Yes. Several long-term care insurance companies have gone bankrupt or simply stopped selling LTC insurance. Of course, it's important to deal with top-rated companies, but even some top-rated companies have gotten out of the long-term care insurance business in recent years, so buying these policies definitely involves some degree of risk.

CHAPTER 18

VETERANS AID AND ATTENDANCE

The Department of Veterans Affairs pays for long-term care primarily through its "Aid and Attendance" payments, which is actually a special pension with an add-on for Aid and Attendance. The eligibility requirements based on periods of wartime are:

- **World War II**: December 7, 1941, through December 31, 1946
- **Korean Conflict**: June 27, 1950, through January 31, 1955
- **Vietnam Era**: August 5, 1964, through May 7, 1975; for veterans who served "in country" before August 5, 1964: February 28, 1961, through May 7, 1975
- **Current Era**: August 2, 1990, through a date to be set by law or presidential proclamation

To be an eligible veteran, you must have served ninety days active duty, at least one day during a period of war, and must have not been dishonorably discharged. If you entered active duty after September 7, 1980, generally you must have served at least twenty-four months or the full period for which called or ordered to active duty, and at least one day has to have been during a war-time period (though there are exceptions to this rule). For a veteran's surviving spouse to be eligible, the surviving spouse must have been married for at least one year to the veteran at the time of death or had children with the veteran. Divorce or remarriage excludes qualification.

MEDICAL QUALIFICATION

Once you are determined to be an eligible veteran, the next question is whether you are medically qualified. If you are age sixty-five and older, there is no requirement to prove disability. However, you or your spouse must be in need of regular aid and attendance due to specific criteria:

- inability to dress or undress yourself, or to keep yourself ordinarily clean and presentable;
- frequent need of adjustment of any special prosthetic or orthopedic appliances that, by reason of the particular disability, cannot be done without aid (this will not include the adjustment of appliances that normal persons would be unable to adjust without aid, such as supports, belts, lacing at the back, etc.);
- inability to feed yourself through loss of coordination of upper extremities or through extreme weakness;
- inability to attend to the wants of nature; or
- incapacity, physical or mental, that requires care or assistance on a regular basis to protect you from hazards or dangers incident to your daily environment.

Not all of the disabling conditions in the preceding list are required to exist. It is only necessary that the evidence establish that you or your spouse needs "regular" (scheduled and ongoing) aid and attendance from someone else, not that there be a twenty-four-hour need.

If you are not at least sixty-five years of age or older, then you must be an individual who is permanently and totally disabled (not due to your own willful misconduct), a patient in a nursing home, or a recipient of Social Security Disability benefits.

Determinations of a need for the Aid and Attendance benefit is based on medical reports and findings by private physicians or from hospital facilities. Authorization of Aid and Attendance benefit is automatic if evidence establishes the claimant is a patient in a nursing home or that the claimant is blind or nearly blind or having severe visual problems.

NET WORTH QUALIFICATION

There is no set limit on how much net worth a veteran and his or her dependents can have to qualify financially for the Aid and Attendance benefit. According to the Department of Veterans Affairs, "net worth cannot be excessive." Unfortunately, the VA does not define "excessive," but rather makes the vague and sweeping statement that the decision as to whether a veteran's net worth is "excessive" depends on the facts of each individual case. The VA says it looks at all of the claimant's assets and determines "if a veteran's assets are of a sufficient amount that the claimant could live off these assets for a reasonable period of time."

In my practice, I have found that a reasonable amount of money for a veteran to retain to be ensured of receiving this benefit is approximately $10,000. For veterans with more money than this, there are numerous asset protection strategies that we can employ so that you and your family legally and ethically protect the excess assets.

INCOME QUALIFICATION

Many veterans are mistakenly led to believe that Aid and Attendance is only for veterans with very low income. The website of the Department of Veterans Affairs says that this program is for "wartime veterans who have limited or no income." If you speak to a veterans service representative in a regional

VA office and ask them about the Veterans Aid and Atten-dance benefit, they will ask for your household income. When you tell them your household income, they will compare it to a chart and most often tell you that you earn too much income to receive the benefit. While the information they provide may be technically accurate, what they typically don't explain is the "income" for VA purposes (sometimes called IVAP or "adjusted income") is actually your household income *minus* certain recurring, unreimbursed medical and long-term care expenses. These allowable, annualized medical expenses are such things as health-insurance premiums, home health-care expenses, the cost of paying a family member or other person to provide care, the cost of adult day care, the cost of an assisted living facility, or the cost of a nursing home.

To be able to receive the Veterans pension with the Aid and Attendance benefit, the veteran household cannot have adjusted income (i.e., household income minus unreimbursed medical expenses) exceeding the maximum allowable pension rate (MAPR) for that veteran's pension income category. If the adjusted income exceeds MAPR, there is no benefit. If adjusted income is less than the MAPR, the veteran receives a pension income that is equal to the difference between MAPR and the household income adjusted for unreimbursed medical expenses. The pension income is calculated based on twelve months of future household income, but paid monthly.

MAXIMUM BENEFIT

As of 2017, the maximum possible benefit (i.e., the maximum MAPR) for the Aid and Attendance benefit is as follows:

- **Single Veteran**: ~$21,531 per year ($1,794 per month)
- **Married Veteran**: ~$25,525 per year ($2,127 per month)
- **Surviving Spouse**: ~$13,836 per year ($1,153 per month)

- **Married Veterans both with need**: ~$34,153 per year ($2,846 per month)

HOW IS THE BENEFIT CALCULATED?

The monthly award is based on VA calculation of twelve months of estimated future income and subtracting from that twelve months of estimated future, recurring, and predictable medical expenses. Allowable medical expenses are reduced by a deductible to produce an adjusted medical expense that, in turn, is subtracted from the estimated twelve months of future income.

The net income derived from subtracting adjusted medical expenses from income is called "countable" income, or IVAP (income for Veterans Affairs purposes). This countable income is then subtracted from the maximum allowable pension rate (MAPR), and that result is divided by twelve to determine the monthly income pension award. Medical expenses must exceed income by 5 percent for the maximum benefit. This award is paid in addition to the family income that already exists.

Examples of Benefit Calculations

Assume two veterans living in the same assisted living facility both having the same supplemental health insurance, one with retirement income of $4,880 per month and the other with retirement income of $4,642.70 per month.

Here's the calculation of the countable unreimbursed monthly medical expenses for both veterans:

Assisted Living Facility	$4,500.00
Plus Medicare Part B	$99.90
Plus Medicare Supplemental Insurance	$128.00
Equals Total Monthly Unreimbursed Medical Expenses	$4,727.90
Minus 5% of Maximum Benefit ($1,794)	$-89.70

Equals Countable Unreimbursed Monthly Medical Expenses	$4,638.20

Here's the calculation of the IVAP and the total Aid and Attendance benefit per month for the first veteran:

Total Monthly Income	$4,880.00
Less Countable Unreimbursed Medical Expenses	$-4,638.20
Equals IVAP	$241.80
Maximum Aid and Attendance Benefit	$1,794.00
Less IVAP	$-241.80
Equals Total Aid and Attendance Benefit per Month	$1,552.20

Here's the calculation of the IVAP and the total Aid and Attendance benefit per month for the second veteran:

Total Monthly Income	$4,642.70
Less Countable Unreimbursed Medical Expenses	$-4,638.50
Equals IVAP	$4.20
Maximum Aid and Attendance Benefit	$1,794.00
Less IVAP	$4.20
Equals Total Aid and Attendance Benefit per Month	$1,789.80

CHAPTER 19

MEDICAID BASICS

A society will be judged on how it treats those in the dawn of life,
those in the twilight of life, and those in the shadow of life.
—Hubert Humphrey

There are many different types of Medicaid, but the Medicaid that will be discussed in this book is the governmental benefits program that pays for Americans who need custodial long-term care, typically provided in nursing homes. Medicaid is funded by federal and state taxes and administered by each state. While the rules for eligibility vary from state to state, the primary benefit of Medicaid is that it will pay for long-term care in a nursing home once an individual has qualified. As mentioned previously, according to AARP, about 70 percent of nursing home residents are supported, at least in part, by Medicaid. Most important, long-term care paid for by the Medicaid program is legally required to be of the same quality as that of a private-pay patient.

The current societal crisis posed by the increasing need for long-term care is a relatively new one. Prior to the advent of nursing homes in the 1950s, those seniors who lived into old age were typically cared for in the homes of their children. Life expectancy was such that most people died before the advent of chronic diseases such as Alzheimer's. Healthier lifestyles and advances in modern medicine have been causing Americans to live longer and longer. Unfortunately, this increased life expectancy means that Americans are often outliving their ability to care for themselves.

Many Americans falsely believe that Medicare will provide chronic/custodial care for themselves and their parents. These people are shocked when they learn the truth: that Medicaid, not Medicare, is the only governmental benefit available to pay for long-term care.

Medicaid, created in 1965 under President Lyndon Johnson, has effectively become the long-term care insurance of the middle class because of the simple fact that very few people can afford to pay the national average of $90,520 per year for a private room or even the $81,030 per year for a semiprivate room.[1] As the primary source of nursing home funding in the United States, Medicaid is one of the federal government's three "social contracts" with America—the other two being Social Security (which provides retirement income for older Americans) and Medicare (which provides health-care coverage).

In 2005, Senator Jay Rockefeller, then the ranking member of the Senate Finance Committee's Subcommittee on Health Care, in marking the fortieth anniversary of the Medicaid program, stated:

> President Johnson's noble concept was not just a Democratic
> ideal; it had been an inspiration shared throughout the early
> part of the century by legislators and presidents from both par-

---

[1] "The MetLife Market Survey of Nursing Home, Assisted Living Costs, Adult Day Services, and Home Care Costs." October 2011. http://www. metlife.com/mmi/research/2011-market-survey-long-term-care-costs.html

ties. And since the signing of the landmark legislation, administrations—both Republican and Democratic—have fought to preserve the Medicaid mission of providing healthcare for the nation's most vulnerable citizens.

Sadly, in the past few years, we have seen a misguided, darker view of Medicaid emerge—one that loses sight of its original goal and underlying moral framework. Medicaid has become a scapegoat for the larger ills facing our entire healthcare system. But Medicaid isn't the problem . . . Taking care of our most vulnerable people is a moral obligation.

Our representative democracy has a responsibility to do for the future what we have repeatedly done in the past: protect, preserve, and strengthen Medicaid

APPLYING FOR MEDICAID—WHY YOU NEED HELP

Sixteen years after the creation of Medicaid, the United States Supreme Court called the Medicaid laws "an aggravated assault on the English language, resistant to attempts to understand it" (*Schweiker v. Gray Panthers*, 453 US 34, 43 [1981]). Thirteen years later, the United States Court of Appeals for the Fourth Circuit called the Medicaid Act one of the "most completely impenetrable texts within human experience" and "dense reading of the most tortuous kind" (*Rehabilitation Association of Va. v. Kozlowski*, 42 F.3d 1444, 1450 [4th Cir. 1994]). Since then, it has only gotten worse.

Congress enacted the Deficit Reduction Act of 2005 on June 23, 2006, retroactive to February 8, 2006, the date of enactment, which rewrote a huge portion of the Medicaid law.

The actual Medicaid application process differs from state to state, but it typically involves filling out a lengthy and detailed application and also submitting appropriate verifications of income, assets, transfers, identity, and citizenship.

Due to the tremendous complexity of the Medicaid laws, the Medicaid application process is also extremely complicated, and many persons who file for Medicaid without professional assistance will wind up with the application being rejected for a variety of reasons. Rejection often occurs due to financial issues—either excess resources, excess income, or improperly timed gifts or transfers. In many cases, rejection is due to missing or incomplete information or verifications. Applications are also sometimes improperly rejected by an eligibility worker (most of whom are underpaid and overworked) who has not had the time to carefully and thoroughly review the application and verifications, or who has improperly applied the legal or financial requirements for eligibility.

Worse yet, an application that is filed at the wrong time can result not only in rejection, but in the imposition of significant penalties against the applicant that could have been avoided by a more timely filing. For these and many other reasons, an experienced elder law attorney should always be hired to represent the applicant through the entire Medicaid process—including planning for eligibility (including, if necessary, Medicaid asset protection), preparing and filing the application, working with the local eligibility department during the application and verification process, filing an appeal when necessary, and representing the applicant in connection with any required hearings and appeals.

WHO CAN GET LONG-TERM CARE MEDICAID?

Almost anyone can get long-term care Medicaid, also sometimes called "middle-class Medicaid." This type of Medicaid is not a program for poor people. It is a program for anyone who can meet the eligibility criteria. Those criteria will be explained in detail in the next several sections.

OVERVIEW OF MEDICAID ELIGIBILITY CRITERIA

There are four separate but overlapping eligibility criteria for long-term care Medicaid (hereinafter referred to solely as "Medicaid"): medical, resource, income, and transfer.

Medical Eligibility

In most states, to be eligible for Medicaid long-term care assistance, you must generally be "medically needy"—meaning in need of a nursing home level of care, though some states have expanded Medicaid to cover the assisted living level of care. Determination of eligibility for long-term medical care is typically based on a comprehensive needs assessment, which must demonstrate that the proposed Medicaid recipient requires nursing facility services. This individual may have unstable medical, behavioral, and/or cognitive conditions, one or more of which may require ongoing nursing assessment, intervention, and/or referrals to other disciplines for evaluations and appropriate treatment. Often, adult nursing-facility residents have severe cognitive impairments and related problems with memory deficits and problem-solving. These impairments and deficits severely compromise personal safety and, therefore, require a structured, therapeutic environment. Most nursing facility residents are also dependent on others in several activities of daily living (walking, transferring, feeding, dressing, bathing, and toileting).

Resource Eligibility

In every state, an individual applicant for Medicaid long-term care assistance may have no more than a small amount in "countable resources" in his or her name in order to be "resource eligible" for Medicaid. For example, in Virginia, this individual resource allowance is $2,000. A married couple both applying for Medicaid long-term care assistance may have no more than $3,000 total resources allowance in their names in order to be resource eligible for Medicaid.

Exempt Assets and Countable Assets

To qualify for Medicaid, applicants must pass some very strict tests on the type and amount of assets they can keep. To understand how Medicaid works, one first needs to learn to differentiate what are known as "exempt assets" from "countable" assets. Exempt assets are those that Medicaid does not take into account. In most states, that includes:

- The applicant's principal residence so long as the equity is below the home equity cap, which is currently $552,000 in most states, but as high as $828,000 or more in some states, and is indexed for inflation. However, in some states, such as Virginia, after the nursing home resident has been in the nursing home for a period of time (e.g., six months in Virginia), the resident's home will become a countable resource unless the resident's spouse or other dependent relatives live in the home. When the home is an exempt resource, that means the Medicaid applicant can keep the home and still qualify for Medicaid. But it also means that the home will be part of the Medicaid recipient's estate at death and that the state can therefore exercise Estate Recovery (see page 129) against the home after death, thereby recovering from the sales proceeds of the home some or all of what Medicaid paid during the lifetime of the Medicaid recipient.

- Personal possessions, such as clothing, furniture, and jewelry

- One motor vehicle, without regard to value

- Certain property used in a trade or business

- Certain prepaid burial arrangements

- Term life insurance policies with no cash value

- A life estate in real estate (however, the transfer rules on life estates are very complicated and must be carefully observed). Also, in some states, retention of a life estate means that the actuarial value of the life estate immediately prior to death will be considered to be part of the Medicaid recipient's estate at death and that the state can therefore exercise Estate Recovery against the home after death, thereby recovering from the sales proceeds of the home some or all of what Medicaid paid during the lifetime of the Medicaid recipient.

- Certain special needs trusts
- Certain assets that are considered inaccessible for one reason or another

All other assets are generally "countable" assets, technically called "resources." Basically all money and property, and any item that can be valued and turned into cash, is a countable asset. This generally includes:

- Cash, savings and checking accounts, credit union share, and draft accounts
- Certificates of deposit
- Individual retirement accounts (IRAs), Keogh plans, 401(k) and 403(b) accounts (though some states exempt retirement accounts if they are in some sort of "payout" status, even though they have a cash value)
- Nursing home accounts
- Prepaid funeral contracts that can be canceled
- Certain trusts (depending on the terms of the trust)
- Real estate other than the primary residence
- Any additional motor vehicles
- Boats or recreational vehicles
- Stocks, bonds, or mutual funds
- Land contracts or mortgages held on real estate

Estate Recovery Rules

Under federal regulations and state laws, the Medicaid agency of every state may make a claim against a deceased Medicaid recipient's estate when the recipient was age fifty-five or over. The recovery can include any Medicaid payments made on his or her behalf. This claim can be waived if there are surviving dependents. One of the goals of Medicaid asset protection, discussed later in this book, is to prevent estate recovery.

Income Eligibility

Most people mistakenly think that Medicaid is only for people with very low income. The actual rule for income is that a Medicaid applicant can qualify so long as his gross income is less than the private-pay cost of the nursing home care he is receiving. A Medicaid recipient must pay all of his income, less certain deductions, to the nursing home. The deductions include a small monthly personal needs allowance, which ranges from around $40 per month to $100 per month depending on the state; a deduction for certain uncovered medical expenses (such as medical insurance premiums); and, in the case of a married applicant, an allowance (called the community spouse resource allowance), which the nursing home spouse may possibly be able to pay to the spouse who continues to live at home. See the following page for more information about the community spouse resource allowance and other protection for the community spouse.

Some states are "medically needy" states and some states are "income cap" states. In "income cap" states, a Medicaid applicant must have income lower than a specified "cap." However, in those states a special trust, called a Miller trust (also called a qualifying income trust, a qualified income trust, an income cap trust, or an income assignment trust), is needed if the Medicaid applicant's income is above a certain level. The way the Miller trust works is that after the trust is created, the patient assigns his or her right to receive social security and pension to the trust. In the eyes of the state Medicaid agency, if the Miller trust is receiving income, the patient is not receiving that income, and thus the excess income "problem" is solved.

The Look-Back Period and the Transfer Rules

The look-back period for Medicaid is five years from the date of application. This means that when you file an application for Medicaid, you are asked whether you made any gifts (including charitable donations) or other uncompensated transfers during the five years prior to applying for Medicaid. Uncompensated transfers include things such as gambling losses and paying money for someone else's benefit, such as paying for a child's wedding or putting money into a fund for a grandchild's education.

Uncompensated Transfers and Penalty Periods

When you file an application for Medicaid, you are asked whether you made any gifts (including charitable donations) or other uncompensated transfers during the five years prior to applying for Medicaid.

Transfer Penalty

An uncompensated transfer of assets results in a period of ineligibility for Medicaid, typically called a "penalty period." The penalty period begins when (a) the person would be receiving an institutional level of care, (b) an application has been filed, and (c) a person is not in any other period of ineligibility. For most people, this means at the time an application is filed and they are receiving care. It is important to understand that the transfer penalty period can be longer than five years. Some examples of how the penalty period is calculated are shown in the following chart:

Hypothetical State Penalty Divisor			=	$8,000
Amount Transferred	÷	8000	=	Penalty Period
$100,000.00	÷	8000	=	12.5 Months
$150,000.00	÷	8000	=	18.8 Months
$250,000.00	÷	8000	=	31.3 Months
$500,000.00	÷	8000	=	62.5 Months

PROTECTIONS FOR THE COMMUNITY SPOUSE

Federal law provides some basic built-in protection for married couples. This law recognizes that it is not fair to completely impoverish both spouses when only one spouse needs to qualify for Medicaid nursing home care.

Community Spouse Resource Allowance (CSRA)

All countable assets owned by a married couple as of the "snapshot date" (the first day of the first month that the Medicaid applicant enters the nursing home or becomes "institutionalized," meaning a resident of a hospital and/or nursing home for more than thirty continuous days), regardless of whether titled jointly or in the name of just one spouse, are divided into equal halves. One-half of the countable assets (subject to a current maximum under federal law of $120,900 and minimum of $24,180[1]) is then allocated to the community spouse. This amount that is allocated to the community spouse is called the "community spouse resource allowance," or CSRA (sometimes called the "protected resource amount," or PRA). The remaining assets are allocated to the nursing home spouse and must be reduced until only the individual resource allowance remains, at which time the nursing home spouse will qualify for Medicaid. The following examples assume a state with a $2,000 individual resource allowance.

- Example 1: John and Mary have $100,000 in combined resources just prior to the date John enters the nursing home. John will be eligible for Medicaid once the couple's combined assets have been reduced to $52,000 ($2,000 individual resource allowance for John plus $50,000 for Mary as her community spouse resource allowance).

---

[1] These amounts are as of Jan. 1, 2017, and are subject to change annually; for updated numbers on every state, see http://www.elderlawanswers.com. Some states are more generous and have a higher minimum CSRA, and some always allow the community spouse to retain the maximum CSRA, even if it is more than half of the snapshot amount.

- Example 2: Bill and Nancy have $200,000 in combined resources just prior to the date Nancy enters the nursing home. Nancy will be eligible for Medicaid once the couple's combined assets have been reduced to $122,900 ($2,000 individual resource allowance for Nancy plus $120,900 for Bill as the community spouse resource allowance).

- Example 3: Sam and Jane have $500,000 in combined resources just prior to the date Sam enters the nursing home. Sam will be eligible for Medicaid once the couple's combined assets have been reduced to $122,900 ($2,000 for Sam plus the maximum of $120,900 for Jane as her community spouse resource allowance).

Because states are allowed to have laws that are more generous than federal law, some states automatically allow the community spouse to retain the maximum community spouse resource allowance.

Community Spouse Monthly Income Allowance

Each state allows a possible community spouse monthly income allowance, which is a monthly income shift from the nursing home spouse to the community spouse. Under federal law, the monthly income allowance ranges from the minimum MMNA (monthly maintenance needs allowance), currently $2,002.50 per month, to the maximum MMNA, currently $3,022.50 per month[2], and cannot exceed the maximum MMNA unless a court orders support in a greater amount. The community spouse monthly income allowance is calculated as follows:

---

[2] These amounts are as of January 1, 2017, and are subject to change annually; for updated numbers for each state, see http://www.elderlawanswers.com. Most states use these numbers, sometimes rounded.

Minimum MMNA (currently $2,002.50) + Excess Shelter Allowance

The excess shelter allowance is the amount by which the community spouse's actual shelter expenses[3] exceed the state's "shelter standard" (also called the "housing allowance").

If the community spouse's actual monthly income is lower than the calculated monthly income allowance, the shortfall can be made up from the income of the nursing home spouse. Ideally, this extra income will eliminate the need for the community spouse to dip into savings each month, which would result in gradual impoverishment.

EXAMPLE OF MONTHLY INCOME ALLOWANCE

Assume that Mary is the community spouse, that her sole source of income is $800 per month in Social Security benefits, and that her actual shelter expenses are $988. First we calculate the excess shelter allowance as follows:

Actual Shelter Expenses	$988.00
Minus Shelter Standard	$-551.63
Equals Excess Shelter Allowance	$436.37

Next, we calculate the MMNA as follows:

Minimum MMNA	$2,002.50
Plus Excess Shelter Allowance	$ 600.75
Equals MMNA	$2,603.25

---

[3] Allowable expenses are rent; mortgage (including interest and principal); taxes and insurance; condominium or cooperative fees; and the state's utility standard deduction, unless utilities are included in the community spouse's rent or condominium or cooperative fees.

Since Mary is entitled to a monthly maintenance needs allowance of $2,603.25, but only receives $800, she is entitled to receive the shortfall every month from John's Social Security check; this shortfall is called the community spouse monthly income allowance.

MMNA	$2,603.25
Less actual income	$-800.00
Equals the Community Spouse Monthly Income Allowance	$1,803.25

The community spouse monthly income allowance can be paid to Mary from John's income. The rest of John's income must be paid to the nursing home to partially cover the cost of his care.

CHAPTER 20

THE TEN MOST COMMON
MEDICAID MYTHS

MYTH ONE: GREEDY CHILDREN WANT MEDICAID PLANNING TO PROTECT THEIR INHERITANCE

Reality: If I get the feeling that a child has unduly influenced his or her parent to come visit me in order to preserve an inheritance, I will send them packing. Most elder law attorneys have a passion for protecting the dignity and quality of life of the elder, which is what Medicaid planning is all about.

Reality: The expenses of long-term care caused by a chronic illness are often catastrophic because, in the United States, citizens do not have a right to basic long-term care. Through Medicare, seniors have had virtually universal health insurance coverage for most chronic illnesses since 1965. For individuals under age sixty-five, private health insurance has likewise always covered treatment, medication, and surgery for most chronic illnesses such as heart disease, lung disease, kidney disease, and hundreds of other chronic medical conditions.

Reality: As previously discussed, our American health insurance system essentially discriminates against people suffering from certain types of chronic illnesses that routinely result in the need for long-term care, such as Alzheimer's disease and other types of dementias; Parkinson's disease and other types of degenerative disorders of the central nervous system; Huntington's disease, amyotrophic lateral sclerosis (ALS), and other progressive neurodegenerative disorders; and many genetic disorders such as multiple sclerosis, muscular dystrophy, and cystic fibrosis. Those Americans suffering the misfortune of one of these diseases must also suffer the misfortune of having the "wrong" disease according to our American health insurance system. Therefore, they do what they can to protect the assets they have built up throughout their lives.

Reality: Medicaid asset protection planning is about fully understanding the existing laws so that we can help our clients keep their dignity and self-worth.

MYTH TWO: A NURSING HOME RESIDENT MUST "SPEND DOWN" VIRTUALLY ALL ASSETS ON NURSING HOME CARE BEFORE QUALIFYING FOR MEDICAID

Reality: Elder law attorneys who specialize in Medicaid asset protection legally help nursing home residents protect significant assets every day. For a married client, we can generally protect 100 percent of their assets, regardless of how the assets are titled, without forcing them to get divorced. For an unmarried client, we can generally protect 40 to 70 percent of the assets.

MYTH THREE: IT IS ILLEGAL TO TRANSFER ASSETS IN THE FIVE YEARS PRIOR TO APPLYING FOR MEDICAID

Reality: Nothing is illegal about transferring your own assets, though there may be Medicaid consequences in doing so.

Many legal and ethical asset protection strategies do involve transferring assets.

MYTH FOUR: ONCE SOMEONE IS IN A NURSING HOME, IT'S TOO LATE TO DO ANY ASSET PROTECTING

Reality: It's never too late to protect assets, even if you, or a loved one, are already in a nursing home facility.

MYTH FIVE: SOMEONE ON MEDICAID GETS LOWER-QUALITY CARE THAN SOMEONE PAYING PRIVATELY

Reality: Disparate treatment between Medicaid recipients and private-pay residents is illegal. In fact, Medicaid recipients who have worked with a qualified elder law attorney often get much better care than their private-pay counterparts because the money that has been protected is often used by a loving family member to help the elder obtain better quality care and to maintain dignity and quality of life.

MYTH SIX: MEDICARE WILL PAY FOR LONG-TERM CARE IN A NURSING HOME

Reality: Medicare only pays for short-term rehabilitation, and only for a limited time and under limited circumstances. Medicare does not pay a single penny for long-term care.

MYTH SEVEN: ALL POWER OF ATTORNEY DOCUMENTS ARE BASICALLY THE SAME

Reality: Full gifting powers must be in a power of attorney (POA) in order to facilitate Medicaid asset protection planning. If you're an estate planning attorney or general practitioner who routinely limits gifting in your POAs, you need to reconsider this practice, which ultimately does a tremendous disservice to your clients.

MYTH EIGHT: A REVOCABLE LIVING TRUST WILL PROTECT ASSETS FROM MEDICAID

Reality: A regular living trust does not protect assets from Medicaid. For a detailed explanation of a living trust that does protect assets from Medicaid, while allowing the settlor the ability to act as trustee and change beneficiaries, see www.livingtrustplus.com.

MYTH NINE: AN IRREVOCABLE LIVING TRUST CAN NEVER BE CHANGED OR REVOKED

Reality: An "irrevocable" trust is a trust that cannot be revoked by the settlor unilaterally. Modification and/or termination can occur by consent between all interested parties.

MYTH TEN: A CLIENT WITH MORE THAN $1 MILLION WON'T EVER NEED MEDICAID

Reality: Nursing homes in my area of Virginia range from about $90,000 per year to over $140,000 per year. A million dollars doesn't go as far as it used to. I've had clients who have spent over $1 million on nursing home care before coming to see me. Long-term care Medicaid is not a program for poor people with low income; it's a program for people who are able to legally qualify under the provisions of applicable laws, regulations, and policy.

CHAPTER 21

PRENEED MEDICAID PLANNING

There are two general types of Medicaid asset protection planning: preneed planning and crisis planning. This chapter will explain the former, and the following chapter will explain the latter.

Preneed Medicaid asset protection planning is for those persons planning well in advance of the need for nursing home care, while they are still healthy and typically still living independently. Generally speaking, these are people who do not have long-term care insurance.

Many people erroneously think they can protect their nest eggs through estate planning using a traditional revocable living trust. Although a revocable living trust does a good job of avoiding probate when properly established and funded, an enormous limitation of a revocable living trust is that it does not protect assets whatsoever from creditors or from the expenses of long-term care. For those wishing to protect their assets from general creditors and from the expenses of long-

ary planning option is the Living Trust Plus
st.[4]

LIVING TRUST PLUS™

...ng Trust Plus™ in 2006, and it's now being used
by dozens of exceptional estate planning and elder law attorneys throughout the country, all of whom can be found listed on the website www.LivingTrustPlus.com. For purposes of Medicaid eligibility, the Living Trust Plus is the *only* type of asset protection trust that allows you to retain an interest in the trust while also protecting your assets from being counted against you by state Medicaid agencies.

Whereas the revocable living trust will protect your assets from probate, the Living Trust Plus is designed to protect your assets from probate *plus* lawsuits *plus* nursing home expenses. You are generally a candidate for the Living Trust Plus provided you are living independently and have no significant health problems that are likely to require nursing home care within the next five years.

Living Trust Plus planning offers you the peace of mind of knowing that the assets you place in trust:

- will be protected immediately from lawsuits and other general creditors;
- will be protected for Medicaid purposes (completely after five years, with partial protection possible in less than five years);
- may possibly be used by your beneficiaries to enhance your dignity and quality of life if and when you need nursing home care.

Whatever assets remain in your Living Trust Plus will, upon your death, be held for your beneficiaries, free of probate, in a

---

[4] *See* http://www.LivingTrustPlus.com.

subtrust designed to protect each beneficiary's inheritance from lawsuits, divorce, and nursing home expenses of the beneficiary.

The Living Trust Plus is an irrevocable asset protection trust that you create as part of your estate planning. The Living Trust Plus allows you to receive all ordinary income from the trust financial assets and to use any trust-owned realty or tangible personal property. The only restriction of the Living Trust Plus is that you can have no direct access to principal (technically called the trust "corpus," which is Latin for "body"). If either you or your spouse has direct access to trust corpus, then all the assets in the trust would be deemed "countable" for Medicaid eligibility purposes and would be completely available to all other creditors. Prohibiting direct access to trust corpus is the key to why the Living Trust Plus works. Because you can't withdraw trust corpus, neither may your creditors.

HOW DOES THE LIVING TRUST PLUS WORK?

Despite the fact that you can't withdraw trust corpus, you have the ability to retain a very high degree of control over the Living Trust Plus assets. In addition to receiving all ordinary income from the trust, you can:

- Live in and use any trust-owned real estate.
- Sell any trust-owned real estate and have the trust purchase replacement real estate if desired.
- Use all trust-owned tangible personal property.
- Sell any trust-owned tangibles and have the trust purchase replacements if desired.
- Drive any trust-owned vehicles.
- Sell any trust-owned vehicles and have the trust purchase replacements if desired.

Additionally, you can:

- Serve as trustee of the Living Trust Plus if desired.

- Remove and replace someone else who's serving as trustee of the Living Trust Plus.
- Change beneficiaries of the Living Trust Plus at any time during your life.

IS THE LIVING TRUST PLUS IRREVOCABLE?

Although the Living Trust Plus is an "irrevocable" trust, this simply means that you cannot unilaterally revoke the trust. Despite the fact that the trust is irrevocable, it can still be terminated as long as the trustee and all beneficiaries agree to terminate it. Many people, including many misinformed attorneys, erroneously think that the term "irrevocable" means the trust can never be revoked. But, in actuality, the term "irrevocable" means just one thing: the trust cannot be unilaterally revoked by the trust creator. Although the Living Trust Plus is irrevocable and can't be revoked unilaterally by the trust creator, under common law and under the Uniform Trust Code, this type of irrevocable trust can be modified, revoked, or partially revoked upon the consent of all interested parties, which is the trust creator, the trustee, and all trust beneficiaries.

WHAT IF I NEED SOME OF THE TRUST CORPUS?

Although direct withdrawal of trust corpus from the Living Trust Plus is prohibited, there's the potential to indirectly access the trust corpus in two ways. The first way is that the trustee has the ability to make distributions of trust corpus to the trust beneficiaries, who are typically your adult children. If the trustee distributes corpus to a trust beneficiary, that beneficiary can then voluntarily (without any prearrangement) return some or all of that corpus or use some or all of that corpus for your benefit. The second way for the settlor to possibly get at the trust corpus is for the trust to be terminated by the agreement of all interested parties as just explained.

Also, the Living Trust Plus is designed to permit the trustee to make distributions to beneficiaries. Through this mechanism the trustee can stop income payments to a settlor who will be requiring Medicaid and can avoid estate recovery in those states that use a broad definition of "estate."

WHAT KIND OF ASSETS SHOULD LIVING TRUST PLUS OWN?

The main types of assets that can be protected using the Living Trust Plus are real estate, including your primary residence; financial investments; ordinary bank accounts; and any life insurance that has cash value. Qualified retirement plans can't be owned by a trust, so to be protected they must first be liquidated and subjected to taxation. This is not necessarily a bad thing if you are over age 59½. Regardless of your political persuasion, congress agreeing to keep taxes low while we are experiencing the highest debt and deficit in our country's history is implausible. Higher taxes are inevitably in our future until our country gets spending under control. Cash value in your retirement accounts is, in most states, a countable asset for Medicaid, so to protect those assets by putting them into the Living Trust Plus, they must be liquidated and subject to taxation. You can liquidate your retirement accounts now, while taxes are at historic lows, or wait until later and risk that the government will have changed the tax rate you have to pay when you withdraw the money. And don't forget that you *will* have to pay tax on this money at some point. In fact, when you turn 70½, the government will force you to start taking at least the required minimum distribution (RMD) each year and pay the prevailing tax rates at that time. The Living Trust Plus doesn't affect your retirement income or your primary checking account.

If you are adamantly opposed to liquidating your IRA or other retirement accounts and paying the income taxes now in order to take full advantage of the Living Trust Plus, then please know that there are other strategies that can be used to protect your assets and still help pay for long-term care.

These are financial strategies such as long-term care insurance or hybrid products such as life insurance products or annuity products that offer long-term care benefits. In fact, there are ways that you can use money from your IRA or other qualified retirement accounts to help pay for these products on a tax-free basis under the rules allowed by the Pension Protection Act. The Pension Protection Act of 2006 (PPA) actually encourages the purchase of long-term care insurance by allowing policyholders to take tax-free distributions from their life and annuity policies to pay their long-term care insurance premiums.

THE REASONS FOR USING THE LIVING TRUST PLUS

Medicaid Asset Protection

We live during a time when many baby boomers are taking care of their own parents and children and consequently putting off planning for their own retirement and long-term care solutions. Furthermore, there are many Americans who can't qualify for long-term care insurance, and these are the ideal candidates for use of the true asset protection capabilities embodied by the Living Trust Plus asset protection trust.

The typical clients who use the Living Trust Plus are in their mid-sixties to mid-eighties, already retired, and worried about the potential catastrophic cost of long-term care. They want to protect the nest egg that they've been saving for a rainy day.

Of course, as a Certified Elder Law Attorney, I know that the rainiest day possible is the day you wind up in a nursing home, so if you want to truly protect your nest egg and have it actually benefit you when the time comes, you need to do something to protect that money. For the vast majority of Americans, the Living Trust Plus is the best way to get this much-needed protection.

The Living Trust Plus is a means by which you can transfer the assets you wish to protect to a trust rather than directly to your children. Transfers to trusts can be rightfully viewed as protection, whereas transfers to adult children are outright gifts. Trusts provide a sense of dignity and security; gifts to children leave you at the mercy of your children and any future creditors of your children. Transfers to a Living Trust Plus are subject to the Medicaid five-year look-back period previously discussed on page 130.

Independence

By transferring assets to a Living Trust Plus, income is paid directly to you rather than to your children, allowing you to maintain greater financial independence. When your real estate is transferred to a Living Trust Plus, you retain the ability to live in the real estate or receive the rental income from the property.

Risk Avoidance

If a parent transfers assets directly to his children, certain risks must be anticipated: creditors' claims against a child; divorce of a child; bad habits of a child; need for financial aid; loss of step-up in basis.

A transfer to a Living Trust Plus avoids all of these risks.

TAXATION ISSUES RELATING TO THE LIVING TRUST PLUS

Income Tax

Because all trust income flows through the trust to the settlor (also called the grantor), the Living Trust Plus is considered by the IRS to be a "grantor trust." Therefore, the ordinary income of the trust is paid directly to the settlor of the trust, and the tax will be paid at the settlor's tax rate, rather than by the trust at the compressed trust tax rates.

Income Tax Reporting

The rules for reporting income generated by assets owned by the Living Trust Plus are contained in the instructions for Form 1041, under the section entitled "Grantor Type Trusts." The Living Trust Plus should ideally obtain a separate tax identification number so that potential creditors, including Medicaid, will clearly see the trust as a separate entity. The trustee does not show any dollar amounts on the form itself; dollar amounts are shown only on an attachment to the form (typically called a "grantor trust statement") that the trustee or tax preparer files. The trustee should neither use Schedule K-1 as the attachment nor issue a 1099.

Gift Tax

Because the Living Trust Plus is designed so that the settlor retains a limited power of appointment in the trust corpus, transfers to the Living Trust Plus are not considered completed gifts for gift tax purposes.

Gift Tax Reporting

Even though the transfer of assets into the trust is not considered a taxable gift, pursuant to Treas. Reg § 25.6019-3, a Form 709, US Gift Tax Return, should still be filed in the year of the initial transfer into the trust. On the Form 709, the transaction should be shown on the return for the year of the initial transfer, and evidence showing all relevant facts, including a copy of the instrument(s) of transfer and a copy of the trust, should be submitted with the return. The penalty for not filing a gift tax return is based on the amount of gift tax due, so if there is no amount due, there should be no penalty for failure to file. Nevertheless, a gift tax return should be filed pursuant to Treas. Reg § 25.6019-3. Additionally, the filing of a gift tax return could provide additional evidence to future creditors, including Medicaid, that a completed transfer was in fact made despite the fact that the transfer was not considered by the IRS to be a completed gift for tax purposes.

Gifts from the Trust

Although the transfer to the trust is an incomplete gift for gift tax purposes, if the trustee later distributes trust corpus from the trust to one or more of the beneficiaries, the tax result of such distribution is that a completed gift has now been made from the trust settlor to the beneficiary. Accordingly, a gift tax return should be filed by the settlor for the tax year of such distribution if the amount of such distribution exceeds the annual exemption amount.

Annual Exclusion Gifts

Under the current law (as of 2017), the Living Trust Plus can make an unlimited number of gifts to individuals of up to $14,000 per recipient, per year, and the settlor will not need to file a gift tax return.

Estate Tax

The corpus of the trust is taxable in the settlor's estate upon death under IRC Section 2036, which says that "[t]he value of the gross estate shall include the value of all property to the extent of any interest therein of which the decedent has at any time made a transfer . . . under which he has retained for his life . . . the possession or enjoyment of, or the right to the income from, the property . . ."

Step-Up in Basis

Because the Living Trust Plus is designed so that assets are included in the estate of the settlor, the trust beneficiaries will receive a step-up in tax basis, as to trust assets, to the fair market value of the assets as of the settlor's death.

Capital Gains Exclusion for Sale of Principal Residence

Since the settlor of the Living Trust Plus is considered the owner of the entire trust (including the residence) under IRS grantor trust rules, the settlor is treated as the owner of the residence for purposes of satisfying the ownership require-ments of § 121 of the Internal Revenue Code. Accordingly, by transferring a residence to a Living Trust Plus™, the exclu-sion from capital gains on the sale of a principal residence is maintained.

CHAPTER 22

FREQUENTLY ASKED QUESTIONS ABOUT MEDICAID

Question: Is it *legal* to transfer or retitle assets in an attempt to qualify for Medicaid?

Answer: Yes, it is absolutely legal. There are no laws prohibiting the transfer or retitling of assets. However, transfers must be made very carefully, because a Medicaid applicant who has made uncompensated transfers within five years of applying for Medicaid will face a "penalty period" for Medicaid based on the amount of the transfer divided by the average cost of a month of nursing home care in the applicant's geographic area. See page 131 for a more detailed explanation of how the transfer penalty period is calculated.

Question: If someone transfers assets, when does the Medicaid "period of ineligibility" start: when the transfer is made or when the applicant applies for Medicaid?

Answer: The "period of ineligibility" begins when the applicant applies for Medicaid and is approved for Medicaid but cannot actually begin receiving Medicaid due to the period of ineligibility.

Question: How much of my assets can be protected if I have not done any planning in advance?

Answer: This varies from client to client and depends on the situation and the specific goals and desires of the client and the client's family. In general, if you're married, an experienced elder law attorney can protect 100 percent of your assets, regardless of how the assets are titled. If you're not married, an experienced elder law attorney can generally protect 40 to 70 percent of your assets.

Question: I've heard you can't do Medicaid planning within five years of entering a nursing home—is this true?

Answer: No. This is a myth. As we have already stated, the law imposes a calculated period of ineligibility for certain types of transfers made prior to applying for Medicaid; however, an experienced elder law attorney will be mindful of these laws and will be careful to comply fully with and work within the law, sometimes even making transfers intentionally to create a period of ineligibility. Plus, there are several different planning strategies that can be implemented at any time—even after someone has already entered a nursing home—without triggering any period of ineligibility. Because of the complexities of this type of planning, many of the strategies used and transfers made as part of a Medicaid plan are often very time-sensitive, and you must always be sure to follow your attorney's instructions carefully.

Question: If I added a child's name to my bank account more than five years ago, is it now protected from having to be spent for the nursing home?

Answer: No. The entire amount in a joint bank account is still counted as belonging to you unless you can prove some or all of the money was actually contributed by the child whose name is on the account. Moreover, joint ownership with children can be disastrous for a number of reasons unrelated to Medicaid transfer rules. For example, your accounts, once in joint ownership with a child, will be vulnerable to the debts and liabilities of that child. Thus, if your child is in an automobile accident, your property could be at risk; or if your child has a business setback, runs up large debts, or goes through a bankruptcy or divorce, your home will be at risk. Also, because jointly owned assets will pass directly to the co-owner when you die, and not through your will or trust, titling assets in joint ownership may unintentionally disinherit your other children.

Question: Can't I just give all of my assets away?

Answer: The answer is "maybe"—but only if you do it the right way and at the right time. If assets are given away at the wrong time and/or in the wrong amount, the law provides for a penalty—a period of ineligibility for Medicaid—based on the amount of the transfer. See page 130 for a more detailed explanation of how the transfer penalty period is calculated.

Question: Doesn't federal law allow me to give away $10,000 per year to my children?

Answer: Yes. In fact, the tax limit has gone up to $14,000; as of 2017 the federal gift tax laws allow you to give away up to $14,000 per year to anyone you want. You and your spouse may each give an unlimited number of these $14,000 gifts per year. So, for example, if you have four children and eight grandchildren, you could give away up to $168,000 each year ($14,000 × 12) if you gave $14,000 to each child and grandchild. However, even though the federal gift tax laws allow you to give away up to $14,000 per year to as many people as you wish *without gift tax consequences*, Medicaid laws still apply to these gifts, meaning that these gifts will result in a penalty period for Medicaid. For example, assuming you live in a state with an $8,000 penalty divisor, your $168,000 annual gift would result in a Medicaid penalty period of twenty-one months ($168,000 / $8,000).

Question: Does giving money to my church or other charities create a penalty?

Answer: Yes. Giving away money to charity is treated the same as giving away money to your children or grandchildren. Many people who apply for Medicaid are horrified to discover that they are penalized for having been good stewards and having given money to charities. There is no exception for gifts made to charity, though some states do have exceptions for small amounts that are made on a regular basis.

Question: Are there any assets that can be transferred without resulting in a period of ineligibility?

Answer: Yes. There are transfers to certain recipients that will not trigger a period of Medicaid ineligibility. These exempt recipients include:

1. A spouse (or anyone else for the spouse's benefit)
2. A blind or disabled child
3. A trust for the benefit of a blind or disabled child
4. A trust for the benefit of a disabled individual under age sixty-five (even for the benefit of the applicant under certain circumstances)

Question: Are there any special rules that apply to the transfer of a family home?

Answer: Yes. There are special exceptions that apply with regard to the transfer of a family home. In addition to being able to make the transfers without penalty to one's spouse or blind or disabled child, or into trust for other disabled beneficiaries, the applicant may freely transfer his or her home to:

1. A child under the age of twenty-one (though transferring to a child under eighteen can be very dangerous)
2. A sibling who has lived in the home during the year preceding the applicant's institutionalization and who already holds an equity interest in the home
3. A "caretaker child," defined as a child of the applicant who lived in the house for at least two years prior to the applicant's entry into a nursing home and who during that period provided such care that the applicant did not need to move to a nursing home. Very strict proof requirements are needed to obtain this exception.

Question: Can I really be forced to sell my home in order to qualify for Medicaid?

Answer: Yes. Without proper advance planning, many Medicaid applicants find themselves forced to sell their homes in order to qualify for Medicaid. Fortunately, there are many ways to protect the equity in a home, but because the Medicaid rules are complex and constantly changing, you will need to seek help from an experienced elder law attorney to help you in your planning.

CHAPTER 23

MEDICAID ASSET PROTECTION BASICS

The type of asset protection planning done by most experienced elder law attorneys is known by many names—it is most commonly called "Medicaid asset protection" or just "Medicaid planning" but is also frequently referred to as "benefits-focused asset protection," "long-term care planning," "life care planning," or "chronic care planning."

WHAT IS THE GOAL OF MEDICAID ASSET PROTECTING PLANNING?

The goals that families have for doing Medicaid asset protection differ from person to person and family to family. However, it is most important to point out that preserving an inheritance for children is most often not the goal. On the contrary, generally for a married couple the most important goal is to ensure that the spouse remaining at home is able to live the remaining years of his or her life in utmost dignity, without having to suffer a drastic reduction in his or her standard of living. For a single or widowed client, the most important goal is typically to be able to enjoy the highest quality of life possible in the event of an extended nursing home stay. When there is an adult child or grandchild who is disabled, the primary goal is typically to protect assets to be used for the benefit of that disabled family member who is often also receiving Medicaid and Social Security Disability benefits.

Money that is protected through proper planning can be used to provide a nursing home resident with an enhanced level of care and a better quality of life while in a nursing home and receiving Medicaid benefits. For instance, protected assets can be used to hire a private nurse or a private health aide—someone to provide one-on-one care to the resident—to help the resident get dressed, to help the resident get to the bathroom, to help the resident at mealtime, and to act as the resident's eyes, ears, and advocate.

Money that is sheltered through proper planning can also be used to purchase things for the nursing home resident or disabled child that are not covered by Medicaid—such as special medical devices, upgraded wheelchairs, transportation services, trips to the beauty salon, etc.

Last, a small percentage of clients do have a strong desire to leave a financial legacy for their children or grandchildren, particularly if there is a disabled child or someone who needs special financial help.

UNDERSTANDING EXEMPT ASSETS AND COUNTABLE RESOURCES

To qualify for Medicaid, applicants must pass some very strict tests on the type and amount of assets they can keep. To understand how Medicaid works, one first needs to learn to differentiate what are known as "exempt assets" from "countable assets." In Medicaid lingo, "countable assets" are technically referred to as "resources."

Exempt assets are those that Medicaid does not take into account. This generally includes:

- The applicant's principal residence, but only for the first six months of continuous institutionalization[1]
- Personal possessions, such as clothing, furniture, and jewelry
- One motor vehicle, without regard to value
- Property used in a trade or business
- Certain prepaid burial arrangements
- Term life insurance policies
- A life estate in real estate (however, the transfer rules on life estates are very complicated and must be carefully observed)
- IRS Code d(4)(A) and d(4)(C) special needs trusts
- Any assets that are considered inaccessible for one reason or another

All other assets are generally "countable" assets, technically called "resources." Basically, all money and property, and any item that can be valued and turned into cash, is a countable asset unless it is listed as exempt in the previous list. This includes:

- Cash, savings and checking accounts, credit union share and draft accounts
- Certificates of deposit
- US savings bonds
- Individual retirement accounts (IRAs), Keogh plans, 401(k) and 403(b) accounts
- Nursing home accounts
- Prepaid funeral contracts that can be canceled
- Certain trusts (depending on the terms of the trust)

---

[1] In Virginia, after the nursing home resident has been in the nursing home for six months of continuous institutionalization, the resident's home will become a countable resource unless the resident's spouse or other dependent relatives live in the home.

- Real estate other than the primary residence.
- Any additional motor vehicles
- Boats or recreational vehicles
- Stocks, bonds, or mutual funds
- Land contracts or mortgages held on real estate

An unmarried applicant may have no more than $2,000 in "countable" assets in his or her name in order to be "resource eligible" for Medicaid.

Does this mean that if you need Medicaid assistance, you'll have to spend nearly all of your assets to qualify? No. There are dozens of Medicaid asset protection strategies that can be employed with the help of an experienced elder law attorney. These strategies will be explored in the next two chapters.

CHAPTER 24

REAL-LIFE CASE STUDIES

Though some families do spend virtually all of their savings on nursing home care, Medicaid laws do not require it. As outlined in the prior chapters, the Living Trust Plus™ is designed specifically to protect your family's financial security. In this chapter, we will take you through several real-life case studies. First will be a case study of the typical family who is completely unprepared for the worst-case scenario and does no planning whatsoever. Next we'll take a look at a family who prepared well in advance for a long-term care crisis using the Living Trust Plus asset protection trust. Please note that the following case studies represent "short version" scenarios. The kind of planning discussed in these case studies must be handled in a very precise manner and must always be done with the assistance of a licensed Living Trust Plus attorney.

CASE STUDY ONE: PHIL AND JANET— NO PLANNING

Janet and Phil had been married for forty-eight years when Phil, at age eighty, suffered the first of several strokes. Phil spent two years in and out of hospitals and nursing homes for rehab after each stroke. Each time, Medicare, along with Phil's supplemental health insurance, paid for Phil's hospital and rehab stays because he always first spent at least three days in the hospital prior to going to the nursing home for short-term rehab. Each time Phil was discharged from short-term rehab, Janet would bring him home and take care of him.

Six months ago, the burden on Janet changed tremendously after Phil had his third and worst stroke, which left him paralyzed on his left side and virtually bedridden, with severe brain damage causing about 80 percent loss of his short-term memory. Despite the doctor's recommendation to keep Phil in the nursing home for long-term care, Janet, who is age seventy-two, brought Phil home to care for him because Janet thinks they can't afford the nursing home care, which the nursing home told her is approximately $9,000 per month.

Janet and Phil's assets are their paid-off house, worth about $350,000, and Phil's IRA, which has about $200,000 left in it. As for their income, all they have is their respective Social Security income. Janet knows that Phil could be in the nursing home for many years, and that just two years in the nursing home could wipe out all of their money. If Phil were to be in the nursing home for more than two years, Janet fears she'd have to sell their house to continue paying for Phil's care, and then where would she live? The nursing home admissions director told Janet that after spending all of their money, she could take out a reverse mortgage on their home and use the home equity to continue paying the nursing home, but this option also did not appeal to Janet. Fear and self-preservation kicked in for Janet—she could not help but worry about spending down their limited resources to provide nursing home care for Phil. These emotions were of course combined with love for Phil and a desire to provide him with the best care, which she thought would be care from her, at their home.

What Janet didn't know was that, with the help of a licensed Living Trust Plus attorney, she could have planned years ago to protect all of their assets (the house and money) for herself and gotten Phil on Medicaid very quickly to pay for his nursing home care. Or Medicaid could have been used to pay for professional home health care for Phil, sparing Janet the tremendous burden of caring for Phil herself.

So Janet purchased a hospital bed for Phil and set it up in the family room on the main level, in front of the television. With no concern for her own health, Janet has diligently cared for Phil at home for the past twelve months, but this caregiving has taken a huge toll on Janet, both mentally and physically. In addition to doing the things she's always done—shopping, cooking, cleaning, etc.—among her numerous additional duties Janet now has to change Phil's diapers and his soiled linens several times a day, do at least two extra loads of laundry every day, keep track of and administer Phil's medications, hand-feed Phil the special liquid diet that he must be on to avoid choking, and turn him several times a day so he doesn't develop bed sores.

Unfortunately, Janet had never heard of the Living Trust Plus and instead went to see the estate planning attorney who had drawn up their wills fifteen years ago. All the estate planning attorney did was recommend that Phil sign a power of attorney and advance medical directive naming Janet, and their son, John, as an alternate. He also recommended that Janet sign a power of attorney and advance medical directive naming their son, John, in case something happened to her. The estate planning attorney didn't know anything about elder law or Medicaid or asset protection or the Living Trust Plus, and so he didn't offer any relevant advice in that regard, and Janet didn't even know that there were vitally important questions she should be asking about Medicaid and asset protection.

Because Phil's needs are so severe, Janet has almost no time for herself. Janet doesn't like to complain, but she has mentioned to her only son, John, that she's always tired, she's not able to get out to see her friends anymore, or to go to church (though she happily still mails in her weekly $100 contribution to the church offering to fulfill their annual pledge). She also confides in John that she cries a lot lately, and that she still worries incessantly about running out of money.

Two weeks ago, Janet fell in the bathtub because she was hurrying, as usual, so as not to leave Phil alone for too long. Janet hit her head on the way down and lost consciousness.

Because neither Phil nor Janet was able to call 911, Janet lay in the bathtub, unconscious, for more than a day before their son, John (after calling and getting no answer for the better part of a morning), drove down on his lunch break to check on them. John found his father in his hospital bed, covered in his own feces and urine because his diapers hadn't been changed in almost two days; Phil was also dehydrated because he hadn't been fed during that time. He found his mother unconscious in the bathtub and immediately thought she was dead.

Hysterical, John called 911, and the paramedics were there within a few minutes to deal with the situation.

After determining that Janet was alive but unconscious, the paramedics tried to revive her, but with no success. They transported Janet and Phil to the local emergency room, where Janet regained consciousness after fifteen hours of observation in the ER. Upon regaining consciousness, Janet's pain was severe, as were her injuries—a severe concussion (which would lead to permanent brain damage and memory loss), a fractured right hip, a bone chip in her left hip, and a broken right arm.

Janet was never the same after this fall. Her memory loss from the brain damage was so bad that it mimicked advanced dementia, and the doctors at the hospital said there was nothing that could be done for her memory. They put a cast on her arm and sent her to the local nursing home for recovery and rehab.

As for Phil, after rehydrating him at the hospital, he also was sent to the local nursing home for recovery and rehab.

Unfortunately, neither Janet nor Phil had been admitted for three days or more to the hospital, and neither Medicare nor their supplemental health insurance would pay for the recovery and rehab. The nursing home told their son, John, that he needed to sign the admission documents for both parents and start paying the $18,000 a month private rate, with the first month due in advance. John dutifully did what the nursing home told him, never stopping to consider if there was an alternative because, like his parents, he had never heard of elder law or Medicaid asset protection or the Living Trust Plus.

About three months later, when John realized his parents were going to quickly run out of money, he listed their house for sale. Per the recommendation of the real estate agent, John listed the house for sale at $350,000. The tax-assessed value of the house was $406,000, but the agent said that, in her opinion, the actual market value was between $317,000 and $350,000. When the house didn't sell within two months, John started to worry that it wasn't going to sell before his parents ran out of money, so John decided to buy the home himself for $317,000. To get the money to purchase his parents' house, John had to liquidate most of his retirement account and incur the income taxes and a 10 percent early withdrawal penalty, but he figured this was better than having to pay $18,000 per month for the care of his parents once their money ran out.

John put the proceeds from the sale of his parents' home in their bank account and continued to use this money to pay the nursing home bills.

About eighteen months later, Phil and Janet were still in the nursing home, and all of their money was gone. The nursing home told John he needed to apply for Medicaid for his parents. Without giving a single thought to hiring an attorney or even seeking legal advice, John applied for Medicaid as the nursing home told him to.

The first time John applied, even though he spent more than twenty-five hours over a weekend completing the Medicaid applications, both parents were denied Medicaid because John had failed to fill out the applications properly.

The second time John applied, both parents were denied Medicaid again because John failed to provide the Medicaid agency with all of the documentation and verifications that they requested in connection with the sale of his parents' home and in connection with their charitable gifts, as the agency requested this at the last minute and John did not have time to hunt down and obtain the required documents.

With the help of an experienced elder law attorney, this result could have been avoided. Filing for Medicaid is one of the most complex and nightmarish endeavors in existence and should never be undertaken without first consulting with an experienced elder law attorney. In my firm, we fill out Medicaid applications for our clients every day to avoid the perils and pitfalls that people encounter when trying to file for Medicaid on their own.

An experienced elder law attorney will ensure that all required documentation is provided to Medicaid at the time of filing the Medicaid application, so clients don't have to deal with last-minute document requests.

In the meantime, the nursing home bills were already piling up at the rate of $18,000 per month since Phil and Janet's money had run out, and the nursing home billing department was calling John at home and at work at least once a week, threatening to sue John for the outstanding nursing home bills if he did not make payment immediately. Finally, they turned the outstanding bills ($54,000 for three months of nursing home care) over to a collection agency, which harassed John and threatened to destroy his credit.

At the same time that John was receiving dunning notices from the collection agency, he was being told by the nursing home administrator that his parents were going to be discharged from the nursing home for failure to pay, and that it was John's responsibility to take them home and take care of them, as he had signed the nursing home contracts as the "responsible party" for both of his parents.

The third time John applied, he provided all of the requested documentation, and the Medicaid Agency finally approved Medicaid for both parents but assessed a penalty period of twenty months. This penalty period was incurred because John's parents had made $26,000 in charitable gifts in the last five years, and because John had sold their house for $89,000 less than the tax-assessed value (which Medicaid considers to be equivalent to a gift to the buyer of the home—in this case, John—in the amount of $89,000). The total gifts of $115,000 were divided by the penalty divisor in their state, which was $5,750, resulting in a twenty-month penalty period, meaning a ten-month period of Medicaid ineligibility for each of his parents. This meant that although John's parents had no money left, Medicaid would not pay for their nursing home care for ten months.

Who did have to pay for the nursing home during that time? According to the nursing home, John did, because he signed the nursing contract as the "responsible party" and because he was the recipient of the $89,000 gift in connection with the sale of the home. So John had to pay ten months of nursing home costs for the care of his parents, at $18,000 per month. This was a total of $180,000 that John had to pay as a penalty for trying to help his parents.

CASE STUDY TWO: BRENDA—PLANNING IN ADVANCE WITH THE LIVING TRUST PLUS

Three years ago, Brenda's husband died after suffering a massive stroke. Although Brenda's husband had died quickly and had not needed to spend time in the nursing home after his stroke, Brenda has many friends whose spouses spent significant time in nursing homes prior to their death, and Brenda knows, through these friends, of the financial devastation that is caused by prolonged nursing home stays. Although devastated over the loss of her husband, Brenda is also glad that he did not have to spend any time in a nursing home, because she knows that a prolonged nursing home stay could have bankrupted her.

Although Brenda is eighty-five years old, she is still quite healthy, and able to live independently. The only thing that Brenda can't do is drive, because she has macular degeneration that is causing her eyesight to fail. Luckily, Brenda's oldest daughter, Jane, lives nearby and is retired, so Jane is able to take Brenda where she needs to go.

After the death of her father, one of the first places Jane takes her mom is to the attorney who did their estate planning documents years before her father had died, to see what needs to be done, if anything, about her father's estate. Jane and Brenda are happy to learn that only minimal work needs to be done because all of her parents' assets were titled jointly and would pass to Brenda automatically with proper notification of her husband's death.

Because they are at the lawyer's office, Brenda asks if there is anything that could be done to protect her assets against the possibility that she might someday need nursing home care. (Brenda's primary reason for wanting to protect her assets is to preserve her own future dignity and quality of life; she is not concerned about leaving a large inheritance to her children because all of her children are financially well-off in their own rights.) Although the lawyer is not a Living Trust Plus attorney, he has heard of the Living Trust Plus and suggests that Brenda and Jane look into it as a method of accomplishing the asset protection they are interested in.

That evening, Jane helps Brenda look up the name of a Living Trust Plus attorney by going to www.LivingTrustPlus. com, and they find that the Living Trust Plus attorney in their area is offering an informational seminar the following weekend, so they sign up for the seminar. At the seminar, Jane and Brenda learn all about the Living Trust Plus as a method of

Medicaid asset protection (see page 146 for more information on asset protection) and decide they wanted to pursue it further, so they make an appointment for a free consultation with the attorney.

Once the attorney confirms that Brenda is an appropriate candidate for the Living Trust Plus, Brenda goes ahead and has the attorney prepare one for her, and Brenda also has the attorney transfer her house, which is worth about $340,000 and is her major asset, into the Living Trust Plus. Brenda decides that she will keep her $97,000 IRA, which is her only other significant asset, out of the trust.

For the next four years, Brenda remains relatively healthy and is able to live day to day on her $1,200 per month retirement income plus minimum distributions from her IRA. Jane spends just four or five hours a week helping Brenda pay her bills and balance her checkbook (her dad had always done that before his death) and driving Brenda to her medical appointments. On February 10, six days short of her ninetieth birthday, Brenda trips and falls and breaks her hip. After three days in the hospital and four weeks of rehab in a local nursing home, it becomes clear that Brenda needs to stay at the nursing home for long-term care.

Jane knows that her mom only has about $80,000 left in her IRA, and at $9,200 per month for the nursing home, Jane knows the IRA money will only last about another ten months. Jane returns to the attorney who drew up Brenda's Living Trust Plus to see what can be done.

The attorney explains that Brenda should go ahead and use the remaining IRA money to pay for the first ten months of nursing home care. Although the IRA distributions are subject to income tax, the tax incurred will be offset by Brenda's nursing home bills, which qualify for the medical expense deduction, so little or no taxes will actually have to be paid.

During this ten-month period, Brenda's lawyer explains that Jane, as trustee of her mother's Living Trust Plus, should sell her mom's former residence. The $340,000 or so in proceeds from the sale of the former residence will go into Brenda's Living Trust Plus; and Jane, as trustee, can decide how to invest these proceeds—whether in CDs, mutual funds, stocks, bonds, etc.

At the end of this ten-month period, Brenda will not have any money left to pay for the nursing home. However, the lawyer explains that Jane could then make a "back door" distribution as trustee of her mother's Living Trust Plus of about $16,000 in trust assets as a gift to herself, and then Jane could, if she wishes, voluntarily use that gifted money to help her mother pay for the next two months of nursing home care. Assuming Jane were to do this, then at the end of the two-month period, the Medicaid five-year look-back period will have elapsed, and the remaining $324,000 in her mother's Living Trust Plus will be protected from being counted when applying for Medicaid to pay the remaining nursing home bills for the rest of Brenda's life.

CHAPTER 25

MEDICAID CRISIS PLANNING

Medicaid laws are the most complex set of laws in existence and are impossible to understand without highly experienced legal assistance.

WHAT THE COURTS SAY

As discussed on page 125, the United States Supreme Court has called the Medicaid laws "an aggravated assault on the English language, resistant to attempts to understand it" (*Schweiker v. Gray Panthers*, 453 US 34, 43 [1981]), while the United States Court of Appeals, Fourth Circuit, called the Medicaid Act one of the "most completely impenetrable texts within human experience" and "dense reading of the most tortuous kind" (*Rehabilitation Association of Virginia v. Kozlowski*, 42 F.3d 1444, 1450 [4th Cir. 1994]).

WHAT YOU CAN DO

Get legal help! Without proper planning and legal advice from an experienced elder law attorney, many people spend much more than they should on long-term care and unnecessarily jeopardize their future care and well-being, as well as the security of their family.

WHO SHOULD DO MEDICAID CRISIS PLANNING?

Medicaid crisis planning is for families with a loved one who has already entered, or is about to enter, a nursing home, and it is expected that the nursing home resident will not be able to return home. If this describes your family, you need to know that there are dozens of asset protection strategies that can be used, under the direct and ongoing supervision of a qualified and experienced elder law attorney, to protect your family's assets and obtain Medicaid benefits. This type of planning provides comprehensive Medicaid asset protection, including completion and filing of the Medicaid application and all documents and actions required to obtain Medicaid. When appropriate, veterans benefits planning and the filing of a Veterans Aid and Attendance pension application can also be done. This type of planning provides a client with a written asset protection plan (APP); all appropriate asset protection documents; all research, conferences, advice, expertise, and other services necessary to achieve the desired goals; supervised execution of all documents required under the APP; and unlimited consultations between you and our attorneys and staff as necessary to design and implement the APP consistent with your needs, goals, and desires, and to carry out the APP to completion prior to our filing for Medicaid and/or veterans pension benefits.

HOW MUCH CAN BE PROTECTED?

If you're a married couple and one spouse is healthy and living at home, as a general rule, 100 percent of your assets can be protected for the continued use and benefit of the healthy spouse, regardless of how the assets are titled. If you're not married, as a general rule, 40 to 70 percent of your assets can be protected. In addition to the asset protection, your elder law attorney should assist you when needed with selection of care facilities, review all paperwork prior to signing, and represent you in connection with any threatened discharge from a care facility.

WHAT STRATEGIES WORK?

The asset protection strategies used under this level of planning break down into two broad categories: asset purchase strategies (also called "smart spend down") and asset transfer strategies.

A list of sample asset purchase strategies and asset transfer strategies is provided in the following section.

Sample Asset Purchase Strategies Available in Most States

Prepayment of Legal or Other Services

Paying for the legal services to be rendered by an elder law attorney is a legitimate way for the client to protect assets. Most experienced elder law attorneys charge an up-front flat fee to handle everything that needs to be handled, including preparing an asset protection plan, implementing the asset protection strategies needed under the plan, and applying for benefit. The fee paid by the client to the attorney is part of the money that is effectively being protected.

Payment for Home Improvements in States Where the Home Is Exempt

In some states, the home is an exempt asset in connection with Medicaid, and this is true in all states under certain circumstances, such as when a spouse or disabled child is still living in the home. In these cases, if there are home improvements that would be helpful to the residents of the home, paying for these home improvements is one way to protect assets.

Purchase of a Home (or a More Expensive Home) in States Where the Home Is Exempt

Using the same logic as making home improvements, sometimes it is advantageous to the family to purchase a home or sell an existing home and purchase a more expensive home. For example, an elderly couple might have sold their home and moved to a rental community. If one spouse enters a nursing home, a possible asset protection strategy is for the healthy spouse to purchase a new residence, thus protecting the amount of money invested in the new home. An example of purchasing a more expensive home may be if the parents are living in a small home and need in-home care in order to remain, and one of their children is willing to move into the home with the child's spouse and family and take care of the parents in the home, but to do this the parents will need a larger home, perhaps one with an in-law suite.

Purchase of Household Goods and Personal Effects

In most states, household goods and personal effects are exempt assets, so this is often one way to protect a modest amount of assets.

Purchase Life Estate and Reside for One Year

A life estate is a type of ownership interest in real estate that is noncountable for Medicaid purposes in most states. If the goal is for a parent to move in with a child, a parent can purchase a life estate in the home belonging to the child, and the amount paid will be exempt provided the parent lives in the home for at least one year after the purchase of the life estate.

Purchase of Prepaid Funeral Arrangements

Medicaid regulations permit the ownership of prepaid funeral arrangements if funded totally by an irrevocably assigned life insurance policy and/or by an irrevocable trust that is properly established by a funeral home. The amount of money spent on properly established prepaid funeral arrangements will be protected. In some states there is a maximum amount that can be spent on prepaid funeral arrangements.

Purchase of a New Car

Medicaid regulations permit the ownership of one automobile of unlimited value. If it would be of any benefit to the Medicaid applicant or a family member of the Medicaid applicant, it is often recommended to trade in an older vehicle for a new or newer vehicle, or purchase a vehicle if one is not already owned. This new vehicle could be, for example, a wheelchair-accessible van. The amount of money you spend in acquiring the new vehicle will be sheltered. If neither the Medicaid applicant nor anyone in his or her family has a need for a newer vehicle, in some states the Medicaid applicant can instead purchase a partial interest in a car that is already owned by a family member.

Prepayment of Taxes

If the Medicaid applicant is subject to taxes, such as real estate tax, personal property tax, or income tax, that are not yet due and payable, they could nevertheless be paid early, thereby protecting the amount of money paid.

Payment of Outstanding Debts

Medicaid does not look at outstanding debts except for mortgage debt or debt secured against a vehicle, so you must pay off your debts prior to applying for benefits for those debts to be subtracted from your countable assets. Paying off existing debt, including any mortgages on your home, is therefore a way to protect assets, because by paying off the debt now, you will increase your net worth by the amount of the debt that has been eliminated.

Purchase of a Medicaid-Compliant Annuity

For married couples, the use of a properly structured Medicaid-compliant annuity is a way to protect an unlimited amount of assets in connection with Medicaid. The rules for these types of annuities are very complex and should not be undertaken without the guidance of a very experienced elder law attorney.

Sample Asset Transfer Strategies Available in Most States

Transfer Assets to Blind or Disabled Child

Transferring assets to a to a blind or disabled child, or to a trust for the sole benefit of a blind or disabled child, is an exempt transfer.

Transfer Residence to Caregiver Child

Under the Caregiver Transfer Exception, in most states an individual's primary residence can be transferred to a "caregiver child" without incurring a transfer penalty after that child has provided at least two years of continuous care to the parent in the home during a time when the parent otherwise would have needed to be in a nursing home.

In most states, a statement from a physician and multiple witnesses are required detailing the individual's physical and/or mental condition during this two-year period, why the individual would have needed nursing home health care during this period, and detailing the specific personal and home health-care services provided to the individual during the entire two-year period.

Every state has very strict and exacting detailed requirements for the caregiver transfer exception to be accepted by Medicaid, so this strategy must be done under the supervision of an experienced elder law attorney. However, because of the complex requirements, there is never any guarantee that this asset protection strategy will be successful.

Transfer Residence to Sibling on Title for More Than a Year

In most states, if a sibling has lived in the same home as the Medicaid applicant for at least one year, and the sibling's name was on the title to that home during that one year, then a Medicaid applicant can transfer that home to the sibling without incurring a transfer penalty.

Caregiver Agreement between Parent and Child

When a child is providing in-home care to a parent, the child is entitled to be paid by the parent for that care at a reasonable hourly rate. This requires a contract between the parent and the child, and in most states the need for this contract and the amount to be paid has to be supported by an independent evaluation performed by a third party, such as a geriatric care manager. When a parent pays the child, the parent becomes a household employer, which brings with it numerous required tax withholding requirements and tax filings, and the child becomes a household employee and must report the earnings on his or her income tax return.

Transfer and Cure/Reverse Half-Loaf

This is a very complex strategy that can only be accomplished under the supervision of an experienced elder law attorney and does not work in all states. There are several different ways to employ this strategy, and different methods work in different states, but the key to the strategy is that an amount of money is gifted away, usually to the adult children of the Medicaid applicant. The elder law attorney then applies for Medicaid, which intentionally triggers the start date of the transfer penalty period. Then another amount of money that was set aside is used to pay the nursing home bill of the Medicaid applicant for a certain period of time, thereby shortening the length of the original transfer penalty period, at which time the elder law attorney reapplies for Medicaid.

Medicaid Divorce?

Given the numerous options in most states for protecting assets without having to get divorced, a Medicaid divorce is typically the "last resort" option when doing Medicaid planning for a married couple.

The distribution of assets pursuant to a decree of divorce is not considered a disqualifying transfer. In a Medicaid divorce, the goal is to transfer as much of the assets and income as possible to the healthy spouse to preserve the quality of life of the healthy spouse to the greatest extent possible, while qualifying the nursing home spouse for Medicaid as soon as possible.

What Is a Medicaid Divorce?

The term "Medicaid divorce" means an absolute divorce that includes a court decree that legally divides up the income and assets of the spouses. Some states offer a "limited divorce," such as a "divorce from bed and board," but this type of divorce does not involve a severance of the marital bonds. For a Medicaid divorce to be successful, it must, as a general rule, "end the marriage." Even though a court may determine ownership of property in a limited divorce proceeding, Medicaid looks at the total of all property owned by the applicant and his or her spouse, regardless of how the assets are actually titled. So any type of limited divorce or legal separation that does not result in the end of the marriage will most likely not be considered a divorce under the Medicaid laws in most states.

When Is a Medicaid Divorce Appropriate?

As stated, a Medicaid divorce is typically the "last resort" option when doing Medicaid planning for a married couple. However, there are several situations where a Medicaid divorce may be a good option, or even the best option, and these are discussed here.

In some cases, the healthy spouse might still be relatively young and might have been providing care to the sick spouse for years, and the healthy spouse wants to return to a "normal life" and start dating and maybe even get remarried.

In other cases, the marriage may have already been "on the rocks" before one spouse got sick and needed long-term care. In this case, the healthy spouse might have stayed married for a period of time simply out of guilt and not wanting to be seen as abandoning the sick spouse at his or her time of need.

Another situation when divorce may be the best option is when there's a need to transfer a large qualified retirement account, such as a 401(k), to a healthy spouse using a QDRO (Qualified Domestic Relations Order). A QDRO is a special court order recognized under a federal law called ERISA that creates or recognizes the right of an alternate payee (i.e., the healthy spouse) to receive all or a portion of the benefits payable with respect to a participant under an ERISA retirement plan. A QDRO is a very complex order that includes very specific information and meets very specific requirements and should only be prepared by an experienced divorce attorney.

Another situation when divorce may be the best option is when the sick spouse has income that is too high to obtain Medicaid, especially when the healthy spouse has very low or no income. In this case, a divorce order can award spousal support to the healthy spouse, thus transferring needed income to the healthy spouse and reducing the sick spouse's income to the point where the sick spouse can obtain Medicaid. Certain retirement income must be transferred to a healthy spouse using a QDRO, Social Security income can't be transferred, but a percentage of a federal pension or military pension can be transferred, and 100 percent of most private pensions can be transferred to the healthy spouse by use of a QDRO.

CHAPTER 26

FINDING THE RIGHT LAWYER

Aging persons and their family members face many unique legal issues. As you have read in this book, the Medicaid program and the myriad legal, financial, care planning, and estate planning issues facing the prospective nursing home resident and family can be particularly complex. If you or a family member needs nursing home care, it is clear that you need expert legal help. Where can you turn for that help? It is difficult for the consumer to identify lawyers who have the training and experience required to provide expert guidance during this most difficult time.

Nursing home planning, Medicaid planning, asset protection planning, and estate planning are all services provided by elder law attorneys. Consumers must be cautious in choosing a lawyer and should always carefully investigate the lawyer's credentials.

The most important and most widely recognized credential in the field of elder law is the CELA (certified elder law attorney) designation. The CELA designation is administered by the Board of Certification of the National Elder Law Foundation, which is the only organization accredited by the American Bar Association to certify lawyers in the specialty area of elder law. Among the numerous criteria required for certification, CELAs must pass a rigorous full-day certification examination and receive favorable peer reviews from at least five other attorneys familiar with their competence and qualifications in elder law. CELAs also must have, during the three years prior to certification, handled at least sixty elder law matters with a specified distribution among twelve different areas of elder law and participated in at least forty-five hours of continuing legal education in elder law. You can locate a CELA in your area by visiting www.nelf.org.

The leading professional organization of elder law attorneys is NAELA (National Academy of Elder Law Attorneys), which also has local chapters in most states. Though mere membership in the academy is open to any lawyer and is no guarantee that the attorney is experienced in elder law, NAELA does have a Council of Advanced Practitioners that are highly qualified elder law attorneys who have been members of NAELA for at least ten years and have been voted into membership by other members of the council. You can find a listing of NAELA members in your area by visiting www.naela.org, which will also tell you if the attorney is a certified elder law attorney and/ or a member of the Council of Advanced Practitioners. These members will come up in the listing with CELA and/or CAP after their names.

According to NAELA, the other top-three organizations you may want to call for lawyer referrals are your local chapter of the Alzheimer's Association, AARP, or your local Area Agency on Aging. NAELA suggests you ask lots of questions before selecting an elder law attorney, as you don't want to end up in the office of an attorney who can't help you. Start with the initial phone call. It is not unusual to speak only to a secretary or receptionist during an initial call, but most elder law attorneys do offer a free initial consultation to determine if your issue is something they can help you with. NAELA suggests getting the following questions answered during your first call (or determining the answers in advance by reviewing the attorney's website): Is there a fee for the first consultation, and, if so, how much? Given the nature of your situation, what information should you bring with you to the initial consultation?

In addition to looking for attorneys with the CELA and/or CAP designation and who are members of NAELA, you may want to seek recommendations from any friends and family members who have received professional help with elder law and/or nursing home issues (whom did they use, and were they satisfied with the services they received?). Hospital social workers, discharge planners, accountants, financial professionals, and even other attorneys can also be good sources of recommendations.

Most states and many local bar associations have formal lawyer referral services that can refer you to an elder law attorney. Be aware, however, that many bar association referral services allow new or inexperienced attorneys to join and do not limit the number of attorneys who may join, so if you use a referral service, be sure to check how it operates.

The Internet is obviously another good source of information about elder law attorneys. There are several services that offer independent ratings of attorneys by their peers, including SuperLawyers.com, BestLawyers.com, Martindale.com, and Avvo.com. Look for attorneys with the highest possible ratings. You can also find out a lot about an attorney from his or her own website—most attorneys these days have websites that list at least their educational background and the types of cases they handle, and many attorneys have much larger websites that provide valuable free information, helpful forms, and even offer a way to obtain legal advice online or via email if you are so inclined.

A good example is the author's website, www.FarrLawFirm.com. In general, a lawyer who devotes a substantial part of his or her practice to elder law and nursing home planning should have more knowledge and experience to address the issues properly. Don't hesitate to ask the lawyer what percentage of his practice involves nursing home planning. Or you may want to ask how many new nursing home planning cases the law office handles each month. There is no correct answer. But there is a good chance that a law office that assists with one or two nursing home placements a week is likely to be more up-to-date and knowledgeable than an office that helps with one or two placements a year.

Ask whether the lawyer is involved with committees or local or state bar organizations that have to do with elder law or estate planning. If so, has the lawyer held a position of authority on the committee? Does the lawyer lecture on elder law and/or estate planning? If so, to whom? If the lawyer lectures to the public, you might try to attend one of the seminars. This should help you decide if this lawyer is right for you. If the lawyer is asked to speak at educational seminars to other lawyers about elder law and nursing home planning, that is a very good sign that the lawyer is considered to be knowledgeable by people who ought to know.

In the end, follow your instincts and choose an attorney who knows this area of the law, who is committed to helping others, and who will listen to you and the unique desires and needs of you and your family.

The way to find a Living Trust Plus lawyer is simply by going to the Living Trust Plus website at www.LivingTrust-Plus.com and clicking on "Find an Attorney." There you will find a listing of the dozens of experienced and expert attorneys around the country who have been licensed by Evan Farr and trained in the proper use and creation of the Living Trust Plus asset protection trust.

Unfortunately, there are not yet attorneys in every state who are authorized to offer the Living Trust Plus. However, we are continuously in the process of growing the Living Trust Plus network by adding additional attorneys to work with us in offering the Living Trust Plus asset protection system, and we will be happy to work with you in trying to find an attorney in your local area.

If you are interested in the Living Trust Plus but do not have a local attorney, there is a contact form on the website at www.LivingTrustPlus.com that you can use to contact us, or you can call our toll-free hotline at 1-800-399-FARR and let us know if you have a local estate planning or elder law attorney you have worked with in the past, or a specific local attorney you have identified as someone you would possibly like to work with in the future. If you are able to provide us with the name of a local attorney you would like to work with, then we will be happy to contact that attorney to explore whether we can work with that attorney to provide you with the Living Trust Plus asset protection trust. Or you can direct that attorney to the LivingTrustPlus.com website and have the attorney check out the "For Attorneys" section of the website.

If you have more than one local attorney with whom you'd be comfortable working, please provide us with the name and contact information for each such attorney. If you have not identified any local attorneys with whom you'd feel comfortable, don't worry. We can still try to recruit an attorney to work with us in offering the Living Trust Plus in your local area. In that regard, it would be very helpful to us if you could provide us with a list of each city or town in your state that is geographically close to you.

Once we have obtained the above information from you, we can then start by reaching out to attorneys whose offices are convenient for you to travel to, and we will let you know if and when we have found an attorney with whom you can work.

INDEX

ABOUT THE AUTHOR

Evan Farr, Certified Elder Law Attorney, is the creator of the Living Trust Plus™ Asset Protection System used by dozens of estate planning and elder law attorneys around the country (www.LivingTrustPlus.com) and is widely recognized as one of the foremost experts in the country in the field of Medicaid asset protection and related trusts. Evan has been quoted or cited as an expert by numerous sources, including the *Washington Post, Newsweek Magazine, Northern Virginia Magazine, Trusts & Estates Magazine,* the American Institute of Certified Public Accountants, and the American Bar Association and has been featured as a guest speaker on numerous radio shows, including WTOP and Washington Post Radio.

Evan has been named by SuperLawyers.com as one of the top 5 percent of elder law and estate planning attorneys in Virginia every year since 2007, and in the Washington, DC, metropolitan area every year since 2008. Since 2011, Evan has been named by *Washingtonian Magazine* as one of the top attorneys in the DC metropolitan area, by *Northern Virginia Magazine* as one of the top attorneys in the Northern Virginia area, and by *Newsweek Magazine* as one of the top attorneys in the country.

AV-rated by Martindale-Hubbell and listed in *Best Lawyers in America*, Evan is a nationally renowned best-selling author and frequent educator of attorneys across the United States. As an expert to the experts, Evan has educated tens of thousands of attorneys across the country through speaking and writing for organizations such as his own Elder Law Institute for Training and Education, the National Academy of Elder Law Attorneys, the American Law Institute and American Bar Association, the National Constitution Center, the National Business Institute, myLawCLE, the Virginia Academy of Elder Law Attorneys, the Virginia Bar Association, Virginia Continuing Legal Education, and the District of Columbia Bar Association. His publications include three best-selling books in the field of elder law: *Nursing Home Survival Guide*, which provides valuable information and guidance to families dealing with the possibility of nursing home care and struggling to make the best decisions for themselves or their loves ones; *Protect & Defend*, which Evan authored along with a host of other top attorneys across the country; and *How to Protect Your Assets From Probate PLUS Lawsuits PLUS Nursing Home Expenses with the Living Trust Plus™*. In addition, Evan has authored scores of articles that have appeared in the popular press and dozens of scholarly publications for the legal profession, including two legal treatises published by and available through the American Law Institute: *Planning and Defending Asset Protection Trusts* and *Trusts for Senior Citizens*.

Note: Virginia has no procedure for approving certifying organizations.

Books from Allworth Press

Estate Planning for the Healthy, Wealthy Family
by Carla Garrity, Mitchell Baris, and Stanley Neeleman (6 x 9, 256 pages, ebook, $22.99)

Feng Shui and Money
by Eric Shaffert (6 x 9, 256 pages, paperback, $16.95)

How to Plan and Settle Estates
by Edmund Fleming (6 x 9, 288 pages, paperback, $16.95)

Legal Forms for Everyone, Sixth Edition
by Carl W. Battle (8 ½ x 11, 280 pages, paperback, $24.99)

Legal Guide to Social Media
by Kimberly A. Houser (6 x 9, 208 pages, paperback, $19.95)

Love & Money
by Ann-Margaret Carrozza, Esq. (6 x 9, 248 pages, hardcover, $24.99)

Living Trusts for Everyone, Second Edition
by Ronald Farrington Sharp (5 ½ x 8 ¼, 192 pages, paperback, $14.99)

The Money Mentor
by Tad Crawford (6 x 9, 272 pages, paperback, $24.95)

Scammed
by Gini Graham Scott, PhD (6 x 9, 256 pages, paperback, $14.99)

The Secret Life of Money
by Tad Crawford (5 ½ x 8 ½, 304 pages, paperback, $19.95)

The Smart Consumer's Guide to Good Credit
by John Ulzheimer (5 ¼ x 8 ¼, 216 pages, paperback, $14.95)

Your Living Trust & Estate Plan, Fifth Edition
by Harvey J. Platt (6 x 9, 352 pages, paperback, $16.95)

To see our complete catalog or to order online, please visit *www. allworth.com.*